NATIONAL COUNCIL ON EDUCATION STANDARDS AND TESTING

A LETTER TO CONGRESS, THE SECRETARY OF EDUCATION, THE NATIONAL EDUCATION GOALS PANEL, AND THE AMERICAN PEOPLE

As co-chairs of the National Council on Education Standards and Testing, it is our privilege to present *Raising Standards For American Education*. We believe this report is an important contribution in moving the Nation toward the adoption of high national education standards for all students and a voluntary, linked system of assessments.

Through its deliberations, the Council found that the absence of explicit national standards keyed to world class levels of performance severely hampers our ability to monitor the Nation's progress toward the National Education Goals. We presently evaluate student and system performance largely through measures that tell us how many students are above or below average, or that compare relative performance among schools, districts, or states. Most measurements cannot tell us whether students are actually acquiring the skills and knowledge they will need to prosper in the future. They cannot tell us how good is "good enough".

In the absence of well-defined and demanding standards, education in the United States has gravitated toward *de facto* national minimum expectations, with curricula focusing on low-level reading and arithmetic skills and on small amounts of factual material in other content areas. Most current assessment methods reinforce the emphasis on these low-level skills and processing bits of information rather than on problem solving and critical thinking. The adoption of world-class standards would force the Nation to confront today's educational performance expectations that are simply too low.

Explicit and high performance standards could provide an appropriate yardstick against which students, parents, teachers, and others could measure individual and system progress toward the Goals. This information would also help to better direct the use of resources and time. Explicit standards would provide a common anchor for reforms in such areas as assessment, curriculum, instruction, and professional development, thereby promoting systemic rather than piecemeal reform.

The United States enjoys a unique and complex blend of state and local control of education and national purposes for education. We propose to build on this system by setting in motion the appropriate mechanisms that will result in _local_ commitment to high _national_ expectations for achievement for all students. We do not propose a national curriculum. Standards would provide the basic understandings that all students need to acquire, but not everything a student should learn.

Standards and assessments must be accompanied by appropriate federal, state, and local policies that seek to ensure high quality resources, including instructional materials and well-prepared teachers. The considerable technical and political challenges of going forward are detailed in the Council's report. While fully cognizant of these challenges, we urge the Nation and its leaders to move boldly and decisively toward implementation. We strongly endorse national education standards and a voluntary system of assessments as appropriate focal points in ongoing education reform.

Sincerely,

Carroll A. Campbell, Jr.
Governor of
South Carolina

Roy Romer
Governor of
Colorado

For sale by the U.S. Government Printing Office
Superintendent of Documents, Mail Stop: SSOP, Washington, DC 20402-9328
ISBN 0-16-036097-8

Table of Contents

Cover illustration by Mark Nardini

National Council on Education Standards and Testing

Co-Chairs

Governor Carroll A. Campbell, Jr.
South Carolina

Governor Roy Romer
Colorado

Members

Gordon Ambach	*Council of Chief State School Officers*
Eva L. Baker	*University of California, Los Angeles*
Brian L. Benzel	*Edmonds School District, Washington*
Mary Bicouvaris	*Hampton Roads Academy, Virginia*
U.S. Senator Jeff Bingaman	*Committee on Labor and Human Resources*
Eve M. Bither	*Maine State Department of Education*
Iris Carl	*National Council of Teachers of Mathematics*
Lynne V. Cheney	*National Endowment for the Humanities*
State Senator Carlos Cisneros	*New Mexico Senate*
Ramon C. Cortines	*San Francisco Unified School District*
Chester E. Finn, Jr.	*Vanderbilt University*
Martha Fricke	*Ashland School Board, Nebraska*
Keith Geiger	*National Education Association*
U.S. Representative William Goodling	*Committee on Education and Labor*
State Senator John Hainkel	*Louisiana Senate*
Sandra Hassan	*Beach Channel High School, New York*
U.S. Senator Orrin Hatch	*Committee on Labor and Human Resources*
David Hornbeck	*David W. Hornbeck and Associates*
David Kearns	*U.S. Department of Education*
U.S. Representative Dale E. Kildee	*Committee on Education and Labor*
Walter Massey	*National Science Foundation*
Edward L. Meyen	*University of Kansas*
Mark Musick	*Southern Regional Education Board*
Michael Nettles	*University of Tennessee*
Sally B. Pancrazio	*Illinois State University*
Roger B. Porter	*The White House*
Lauren Resnick	*University of Pittsburgh*
Roger Semerad	*RJR Nabisco*
Albert Shanker	*American Federation of Teachers*
Marshall S. Smith	*Stanford University*

Executive Summary

The National Council on Education Standards and Testing was created in response to interest in national standards and assessments by the Nation's Governors, the Administration, and Congress. In the authorizing legislation (Public Law 102-62), Congress charged the Council to:

- advise on the desirability and feasibility of national standards and tests, and

- recommend long-term policies, structures, and mechanisms for setting voluntary education standards and planning an appropriate system of tests.

The work of the Council follows and complements the President's Education Summit with the Governors held in 1989. This important collaborative effort led to the adoption of six National Education Goals designed to engage all Americans, from young children to adults. The National Education Goals Panel was created to report annually on progress toward the Goals. In its first year, the Panel concluded that to meaningfully measure progress on Goals 3 and 4, consideration should be given to creating national education standards that define what students should know and be able to do and to identifying and

National Education Goals 3 and 4

Goal 3: Student Achievement and Citizenship
  By the year 2000, American students will leave grades four, eight, and twelve having demonstrated competency in challenging subject matter including English, mathematics, science, history and geography; and every school in America will ensure that all student learn to use their minds well, so they may be prepared for responsible citizenship, further learning, and productive employment in our modern economy.

Goal 4: Science and Mathematics
  By the year 2000, U.S. students will be first in the world in science and mathematics achievement.

developing methods to assess students' success in meeting them. The President similarly has called for the creation of World Class Standards for students and high-quality tests on which they can demonstrate achievement of these standards.

In carrying out its charge to examine a broad range of issues, the Council met eight times between June and December, 1991. Task forces were created and produced background papers that informed the Council's discussions. In response to the congressional call for broad public participation, the Council solicited and received public comment from experts and organizations representing a wide range of constituents and interests. This report to Congress, the Secretary of Education, the National Education Goals Panel, and the American people provides recommendations reached after intense deliberation and includes concerns that must be addressed as work progresses on developing standards and assessments.

Desirability of High National Standards and a System of Assessments

In the course of its research and discussions, the Council concluded that high national standards tied to assessments are desirable. In the absence of well-defined and demanding standards, education in the United States has gravitated toward *de facto* national minimum expectations. Except for students who are planning to attend selective four-year colleges, current education standards focus on low-level reading and arithmetic skills and on small amounts of factual material in other content areas. Consumers of education in this country have settled for far less than they should and for far less than do their counterparts in other developed nations.

High national standards tied to assessments can create high expectations for all students and help to better target resources. They are critical to the Nation in three primary ways: to promote educational equity, to preserve democracy and enhance the civic culture, and to improve economic competitiveness. Further, national education standards would help to provide an increasingly diverse and mobile population with shared values and knowledge.

The Council recommends standards for students and standards for schools and school systems. Student standards include specification of the content — what students should know and be able to do — and the level of performance that students are expected to attain — how good is good enough. The Council envisions that the national standards will include substantive content together with complex problem-solving and higher order thinking skills.

To ensure that students do not bear the sole burden of attaining the standards and to encourage assurances that the tools for success will be available at all schools, the Council also recommends that states establish school delivery standards. System performance standards should also be established. School delivery and system performance standards would attest to the provision of opportunities to learn and of appropriate instructional conditions to enable all children to reach high standards.

In endorsing the concept of national standards for all students, the Council stipulates several characteristics these standards should have:

- Standards must reflect high expectations, not expectations of minimal competency.

- Standards must provide focus and direction, not become a national curriculum.

- Standards must be national, not federal.

- Standards must be voluntary, not mandated by the federal government.

- Standards must be dynamic, not static.

The Council's intent in recommending the establishment of national standards is to raise the ceiling for students who are currently above average and to lift the floor for those who now experience the least success in school, including those with special needs. States should work toward reducing gaps in students' opportunities to learn and in their performance, such as those now associated with race, income, gender, and geographical location.

Having reached consensus that standards are desirable, the Council then determined that it is not sufficient just to set standards. Since tests tend to influence what is taught, assessments should be developed that embody the new high standards. The considerable resources and effort the Nation expends on the current patchwork of tests should be redirected toward the development of a new system of assessments. Assessments should be state-of-the-art, building on the best tests available and incorporating new methods. In order to measure individual student progress and to monitor achievement in attaining the National Education Goals, the new system of assessments should have two components —

- individual student assessments, and

- large-scale sample assessments, such as the National Assessment of Educational Progress.

The key features of both components would be alignment with high national standards and the capacity to produce useful, comparable results. In addition, the system of assessments should have a number of other features.

- The system of assessments must consist of multiple methods of measuring progress, not a single test.

- The system of assessments must be voluntary, not mandatory.

- The system of assessments must be developmental, not static.

As these features are put in place, technical and equity issues need to be resolved, and the overriding importance of ensuring fairness for all children needs to be addressed. Resolving issues of validity, reliability, and fairness is critical to the success of the new system.

The Council concludes that the United States, with appropriate safeguards, should initiate the development of a voluntary system of assessments linked to high national standards. These assessments should be created as expeditiously as possible by a wide array of developers and be made available for adoption by states and localities. The Council finds that the assessments eventually could be used for such high-stakes purposes for students as high school graduation, college admission, continuing education, and certification for employment. Assessments could also be used by states and localities as the basis for system accountability.

In the Council's view, it is desirable that national content and performance standards and assessments of the standards be established. Doing so will constitute an essential next step to help the country achieve the National Education Goals. Moreover, developing standards and assessments at the national level can contribute to educational renewal in several ways. This effort has the potential to raise learning expectations at all levels of education, better target human and fiscal resources for educational improvement, and help meet the needs of an increasingly mobile population. Finally, standards and assessments linked to the standards can become the cornerstone of the fundamental, systemic reform necessary to improve schools.

Feasibility of Creating National Standards and a System of Assessments

As a first step, the Council recommends that standards be developed in the five core subject areas set out in the National Education Goals — English, mathematics, science, history, and geography — with other subjects to follow. The feasibility of setting national standards and their effectiveness in prompting state and local reform and experimentation is demonstrated by the work of several national professional organizations, a number of states, and other countries. The experiences of the National Council of Teachers of Mathematics (NCTM) and of several states demonstrate that standards-setting is feasible — it is being done. Slowly but surely across the country, states and local districts are responding to the NCTM standards by changing the curriculum and style of teaching to reflect the challenging new standards. The Council recommends national support for such efforts and encourages the work by professional organizations, states, and localities in articulating standards, curriculum frameworks, and instructional guidelines.

To make national standards meaningful, it is important that the Nation be able to measure progress toward them. New forms of assessments — tests worth teaching to — are envisioned. A system of student assessments linked to world-class standards would provide information that could be used to:

- exemplify for students, parents, and teachers the kinds and levels of achievement expected;

- improve classroom instruction and learning outcomes for all students;

- inform students, parents, and teachers about student progress;

- measure and hold students, schools, school districts, states, and the Nation accountable for educational performance; and

- assist education policymakers with programmatic decisions.

It is unlikely that all of these purposes could be accomplished with the same assessment. Requirements for validity, reliability, and fairness necessitate on-going, independent reviews of the assessments and their uses. Further, particularly for children who have historically experienced less success in schools, such as the poor, ethnic minorities, and students with disabilities, schools should ensure the opportunity to learn as a critical condition for valid and fair use of assessment results.

Some existing assessments may be retained, while others will need to be replaced to avoid adding to the current patchwork. Promising efforts are under way nationally, as well as by states, localities, research institutions, and test publishers using new assessment methods to measure student progress against more demanding curriculum content. Investing in a national system of assessments could lead to more effective and economical use of available resources since it would provide direction and focus to reform efforts. The Council urges support for necessary research and development so that the critical need for assessing students against the yardstick of national, world-class standards can be met.

The Council notes that if they are to be useful, comparable results should be available to all key levels, including individual students and their parents, schools, districts, states, and the

Nation. Assessment outcomes tied to the standards should be widely distributed and communicated in a form that is readily comprehensible to students, parents, policymakers, and the public. States and localities should report results in the context of relevant information on the conditions of learning and students' opportunities to learn.

Developing and Implementing National Standards and a System of Assessments

To ensure that development of national standards and a voluntary system of assessments is done effectively, a coordinating structure needs to be agreed upon and put into place. This structure should benefit from and not duplicate work already being done by existing entities. The Council recommends that a reconfigured National Education Goals Panel and a newly created National Education Standards and Assessments Council work jointly to certify content and student performance standards and criteria for assessments as world class. The Council further recommends that to ensure strong public accountability in this work the Panel would appoint members of the National Education Standards and Assessments Council, which would have the responsibility to coordinate this national effort.

High national standards and a system of assessments, while critically important, are not panaceas for the Nation's educational problems. Other required elements of reform include state curriculum frameworks tied to the standards, professional development opportunities for teaching to the standards, new roles and responsibilities for educators, technology that enhances instructional opportunities, assistance to families and communities in need, incentives to inspire better efforts by students and educators, early intervention where problems are identified, and the reduction of health and social barriers to learning.

Conclusion

The country is engaged in a national debate on what students should know and be able to do and on how to measure achievement toward those ends. This debate is part of a fundamental shift of perspective among educators, policymakers, and the public from examining inputs and elements of the educational process to examining outcomes and results. The Council initially discussed standards and assessments as a way to help measure progress toward the National Education Goals but came to see the movement toward high standards as a means to help achieve the Goals.

While mindful of the technical and political challenges, the Council concludes that national standards and a system of assessments are desirable and feasible mechanisms for raising expectations, revitalizing instruction, and rejuvenating educational reform efforts for all American schools and students. Thus, the National Council on Education Standards and Testing endorses the adoption of high national standards and the development of a system of assessments to measure progress toward those standards.

Part One

Are National Standards and a System of Assessments Desirable?

The Council finds that setting national standards and developing a system of assessments measuring progress toward the standards are desirable. The Council discussed national standards and a system of assessments as a means of tracking progress toward the National Education Goals. Standards and assessments are important tools to help the Nation achieve the Goals by raising expectations and providing information so that available resources can be better targeted. In addition, national standards and a system of assessments tied to them can play key roles in addressing three national priorities. First, they can help us extend the opportunity for a high quality education to all Americans. Second, they can strengthen democratic institutions and values while enabling all citizens to participate more effectively in the political process. Third, they can enhance economic competitiveness by improving the Nation's human capital— the abilities and skills of the country's workers and entrepreneurs.

The Need for National Standards and a System of Assessments

Equitable Educational Opportunity for All Americans

High national education standards and a system of assessments to measure their attainment can play a vital role in raising expectations, especially for youngsters from groups that have historically experienced less academic success. While the Council recognizes that new standards and assessments alone are not a complete education reform strategy, world-class standards and quality assessments can be powerful catalysts for implementing the systemic change necessary to bring all students, leaving no one behind, to high performance standards. The Council has concluded that standards and assessments have the potential to boost the performance of students who are currently above average as well as those who are now the least successful. By emphasizing their applicability to all students, standards and assessments will help assure that adequate resources are available and appropriately targeted to helping all students attain the standards.

To achieve this ambitious purpose, there are three important considerations. First, poor initial performance should not be used to divert students into less demanding courses with lower expectations but rather must lead to improved instruction and redoubled effort. Second, policymakers should seek to ensure that schools provide all their students with opportunities to master the demanding new material in the standards in an atmosphere where achievement is prized. Third, students with disabilities or of limited English proficiency should be provided opportunities to learn and to demonstrate their mastery of material under circumstances that take into account their special needs.

Enhancing the Civic Culture

High-quality national standards and a system of assessments have the potential of helping all students acquire the necessary knowledge, skills, and shared values to deepen and renew our civic culture and of enabling all citizens to participate more effectively in the political processes of democracy. In recent decades, the population has grown increasingly diverse. The Council carefully considered the concerns that standards and assessments might have the effect of homogenizing the culture.

It is the Council's intent that the standards reflect and be enriched by the Nation's pluralistic heritage as well as its shared democratic values and institutions.

Two important considerations have helped shape a number of the Council's recommendations. First, the Council decided that the standards should not be used as a national curriculum. Rather, they should serve as a basic core of important understandings that all students need to acquire, but certainly not everything that a student should learn. States and local jurisdictions need to retain the capacity to include a substantial amount of additional material reflecting their particular interests and emphases. Second, the system of assessments the Council is recommending is not a single national test. Instead, states, individually or collectively, will be encouraged to develop or acquire their own instruments to assess progress toward the national standards. In these important ways, the Nation's legal and historical traditions of state and local control of education are preserved while still developing common ground on key aspects of education that are vital for all Americans.

The United States has historically demonstrated a remarkable ability to bind together a wide variety of groups into one nation. A common understanding of the knowledge and skills future generations of citizens should possess has the potential to serve as a powerful force for national unity, social vitality, and cultural vibrancy.

Economic Competitiveness

High standards for student attainment are critical to enhancing America's economic competitiveness. The quality of human capital, the knowledge and skills of labor and management, helps determine a nation's ability to compete in the world marketplace. International comparisons, however, consistently show that the academic performance of American students is below that of students in many other developed countries. The relative deficiency in America's human capital contributes to the inability of many firms in the United States to compete internationally. Low skill levels may also be impeding American business from shifting to newer, more efficient methods of production that require greater responsibility and skill on the part of front-line workers. These deficiencies likely affect the standard of living of all Americans, but the effects are felt most keenly by those who do not have adequate skills. The Council thus concludes that world-class standards for student performance and a way of assessing progress toward them can be part of education's contribution to addressing the Nation's deficit in human capital and increasing competitiveness in the global marketplace.

The Council finds, as do many in the business community, that standards set in specific academic subject areas should include the type of useful workplace skills described in the U.S. Department of Labor's SCANS (Secretary's Commission on Achieving Necessary Skills) report. In addition to the academic knowledge identified in the SCANS report, skills and personal qualities, such as acquiring and evaluating data, working in teams, monitoring and correcting performance, self-management, solving problems, and knowing how to learn are important for success at work. To the extent possible, these types of skills can and should be integrated into the national standards and assessments. Together with high-quality technical training and the broad knowledge provided by a solid academic education, such skills can go a long way toward creating the literate and competent workforce necessary for a productive economy.

National Standards and a System of Assessments

The Council has come to the conclusion that developing high national standards and a system of assessments measuring the degree to which they are attained has the potential to provide families, educators, and policymakers with the information necessary to make wise educational decisions.

In the absence of demanding content and performance standards, the United States has gravitated toward having a *de facto* minimal skills curriculum. The many state minimum competency tests, the lower level skills orientation of most textbooks, and state and local policies that do not adequately promote quality are examples of this minimal approach. The Council finds that what has been demanded is insufficient in that it covers far too little of the knowledge and skills students need to succeed in the modern workplace and to participate in the democratic process. Such low expectations shortchange students and ill-serve the country. Yet as long as today's low standards remain in place, the performance of the majority of students is unlikely to improve substantially.

Standards developed at the national and state levels should have a number of specific components:

- *An overarching statement* for each subject area to provide a guiding vision of its content and purpose;

- *Content standards* that describe the knowledge, skills, and other understandings that schools should teach in order for students to attain high levels of competency in challenging subject matter;

- *Student performance standards* that define various levels of competence in the challenging subject matter set out in the content standards;

- *School delivery standards* developed by the states collectively from which each state could select the criteria that it finds useful for the purpose of assessing a school's capacity and performance; and

- *System performance standards* that provide evidence about the success of schools, local school systems, states, and the Nation in bringing all students, leaving no one behind, to high performance standards.

The Council concludes that national standards should have the following characteristics:

- *High expectations — not expectations of minimal competency.* The Council noted that educational expectations are currently too low and that, as a result, too many American students perform accordingly. Setting

NCTM Standard 5: Algebra

In grades 9-12, the mathematics curriculum should include the continued study of algebraic concepts and methods so that all students can-

- represent situations that involve variable quantities with expressions, equations, inequalities and matrices;
- use tables and graphs as tools to interpret expressions, equations and inequalities;
- operate on expressions and matrices, and solve equations and inequalities;
- appreciate the power of mathematical abstraction and symbolism;

and so that, in addition, college-intending students can-

- use matrices to solve linear systems;
- demonstrate technical facility with algebraic transformations, including techniques based on theory of equations.

Excerpted from: Curriculum and Evaluation Standards for School Mathematics, *National Council of Teachers of Mathematics. (1985).*

world-class standards will purposefully address this deficiency. Students, regardless of background, will be challenged to meet these high standards.

- *Focus and direction — not a national curriculum.* Standards set would be neither exhaustive nor all inclusive. They should be viewed as a common core that would be enhanced through considerable state and local flexibility. Within the broad framework of the standards, schools and teachers would have the discretion to develop their own detailed curricula, determine subject sequencing, choose materials, select pedagogy, and add content reflecting local and state interests and diversity.

- *National — not federal.* The standards, arrived at through consensus, will be national in character and applicability. It would be inappropriate for the federal government to create or mandate the new standards. Standards-setting must involve the widest possible participation in the process from individuals and groups at the national, state, and local levels, as Congress has noted in the legislation establishing this Council.

- *Voluntary — not mandatory.* Adopting the national standards will be voluntary. The Council anticipates that high-quality standards, developed through a broad and open process, will be widely used.

- *Dynamic — not static.* While care should be taken to develop quality standards from the outset, the process will be ongoing, entailing improvement and refinement over time in order to remain world-class. It is imperative that standards keep pace with the development of knowledge in the subject fields.

To make standards meaningful, the Council has determined that a system of assessing students' success in attaining them is desirable. A national system of assessments should be created that contains two components: student assessments that can provide results for individual students; and large-scale sample assessments, such as the National Assessment of Educational Progress (NAEP). The key features of both components would be alignment with national content and performance standards and the capacity to produce useful, comparable results that are available to all key levels, including students and their parents, schools, districts, states, and the Nation. To assist in developing informed judgments on performance, states and localities should report results in the context of information such as opportunity to learn and relevant conditions of learning.

A national system of assessments should also have the following features —

- *Multiple assessments — not a single test.* It will be up to states, individually or in groups, to adopt assessments linked to the national standards. States can design the assessments or they may acquire them.

- *Voluntary — not mandatory.* State participation in the national system of assessments will be voluntary. The federal government will not require that states adopt any particular tests.

- *Developmental — not static.* The system should be developmental. It should change and evolve over time, maintaining alignment with the national content and performance standards and incorporating improved assessment techniques as these are developed.

Assessments must address important technical issues of reliability, validity, and fairness. Professional standards exist for resolving many of these issues. Particular attention must be paid to the reliability, validity, and fairness of assessment instruments and testing conditions when high stakes for students or educators are attached to test results.

The Role of National Standards and a System of Assessments in Education Reform

A national initiative to develop world-class standards and a system of high-quality assessments that measure progress toward them is vital, for reforming American education, for the following reasons.

American education would be well served by an organized attempt to provide direction on a nationwide basis and to determine some of the important skills and knowledge that all students should master at key stages in their education, without trying to specify a national curriculum. Articulating standards and developing assessments that provide educators and students with targets toward which to marshal their efforts can contribute to more efficient use of available resources. Educators place different emphases on what students should learn at various points in their schooling. In an increasingly mobile society, many students attend a number of different schools over the course of their education, often in different communities or states. Frequently, teachers do not know what they can reasonably expect students to have learned before entering their classrooms and cannot be sure what will be taught afterward. The Council concludes that these educational problems are national in scope and would be addressed best through a nationally coordinated effort. While respecting local and regional diversity, such an effort could take advantage of the useful work already under way in many states and localities, sharing lessons and avoiding unnecessary duplication.

New standards and assessments that provide information useful to improving instruction and student learning would likely be perceived as valuable tools by many teachers. In the absence of national standards, the results from current standardized assessments are sometimes more a source of confusion than a tool for improving instruction. Teachers sometimes feel pressured by the consequences attached to test results to narrow instruction and focus on the minimal skills measured by some current tests. Many of these tests are not designed to guide instruction. The Council notes that recent assessments have explored alternative ways of measuring what students are to learn, and new efforts should build on the important work now under way.

More accurate and dependable sources of information on progress toward achieving the National Education Goals would be an important incentive to change education. The Council recommends that reliable and comparable data on the performance of students against meaningful standards be available to five important levels in education: individual students and their parents, schools, districts, states, and the Nation. Families want and need comprehensible information on students' progress toward high standards. To exercise informed judgment, educators and policymakers similarly need reliable data on student progress in meeting high-quality standards as well as information on other outcomes. The Council concludes that a national effort to set standards and coordinate the development of a system of assessments could provide data that are both high quality and comparable.

The Council further finds a need to shift the basis of educational accountability away from measures of inputs and processes to evidence of progress toward desired outcomes. Given the substantial outlay of public funds on elementary and secondary education in the United States, elected officials and policymakers have understandably been concerned with ensuring that taxpayers' dollars are well spent. Unfortunately, the lack of high standards and quality assessments that measure progress toward them has in the past resulted in accountability being tied primarily to compliance with rules and regulations or to data from assessments measuring only minimal skills. The Council believes that accountability needs to be refocused toward performance. This is especially true where consequences for students or educators are attached to performance on these measures.

The Council finds that a nationally coordinated initiative would result in high-quality outcome measures that can be used for accountability. A national effort would address squarely the necessary technical issues of developing assessments that are valid, reliable, and fair. Unprecedented national attention — by testing experts, educators, policymakers, and the public — could be focused on the system of assessments and use of the results for accountability.

Standards and assessments can serve as catalysts for raising expectations. In many states and localities, the minimum competency skills standards put in place in the 1970s and early 1980s resulted in changes that have helped many youngsters attain at least these low-level skills. The work of the National Council of Teachers of Mathematics to create content standards in mathematics has already influenced the development of state curriculum frameworks and assessments. The College Board Advanced Placement program's course guides and examinations are widely recognized as valuable and useful tools that have helped to provide quality instruction to millions of students across the country. In California, curriculum and assessment reforms are the cornerstone of a strategic education plan that includes changing professional development, instructional methods, textbooks, technology, and other classroom materials.

Setting standards and developing quality assessments of progress toward them should be a national effort. An increasingly global economy requires that national standards be set at world-class levels. Such an unprecedented initiative in this country must find its way through uncharted waters relating to difficult technical and policy issues. Undertaking this effort at the national rather than state or local levels can help to achieve cost-effectiveness and marshal the talent and scarce public resources needed to deal adequately with these issues.

The Council finds a quality system of national standards and assessments embodying the important qualities discussed in this section to be highly desirable. Given that education serves important national purposes, including equitable opportunity for all Americans, enhancing the Nation's civic culture, and improving the economic competitiveness of the United States, and because many of the difficulties of developing high-quality standards and assessments can be addressed best at the national level, the Council recommends a coordinated national effort that respects local prerogatives and diversity in educating students to world-class levels. Such an effort is the necessary next step in achieving the ambitious National Education Goals and has the potential to spur a nationwide process of educational renewal. Rather than threaten local autonomy, standards and assessments can support efforts to improve the quality of education. Standards and a national system of assessments would provide those designing state curriculum and testing systems with a valuable resource developed through a national consensus process. They further provide a focus on improving student performance and could lead to more effective and efficient allocation of resources at the local, state, and national levels.

Part Two

Is it Feasible to Develop National Standards and a System of Assessments?

The Council finds it feasible as well as desirable to create national education standards and a system of assessments linked to the standards. Precedents set by states, localities, professional organizations, and other groups demonstrate that this undertaking is feasible.

Setting Standards in Subject Areas

The process of setting standards is at various levels of development in the five subjects emphasized in the National Education Goals and should be expanded into other subjects, such as citizenship education, foreign languages, and the visual and performing arts. Attention should also be given to developing standards for the application of knowledge to complicated, real world problems that demand integrating student knowledge from several disciplines. The Council recommends that standards be developed through a broad-based process that involves educators, including scholars in each field. Teachers should play a key role in this process. So, too, should representatives of business and the public. The

English in Maine's Common Core of Learning

Students with a common core of knowledge...

- Are familiar with contemporary and enduring works of American literature and have a sense of how important themes of American experience have developed through time
- Are familiar with works of diverse literary traditions — works by women and men of many racial, ethnic, and cultural groups in different times and parts of the world, including Shakespeare, the Bible as literature, and classical mythology
- Communicate clearly — orally, in writing, and with graphics
  - Have a strong command of standard oral and written language conventions
  - Demonstrate basic proofreading and editing skills
  - Use handbooks and reference books to locate language terminology and rules

Excerpted from: Maine's Common Core of Learning: An Investment in Maine's Future.

standards-setting process should be informed by work in other industrialized countries in order to ensure that the new standards are world class.

The process envisioned is a dynamic one with standards updated to meet changes in scholarship and to remain world class. Work that is under way demonstrates empirically that standards-setting is feasible and that the process itself may contribute to educational renewal. The National Assessment Governing Board's process for developing guidelines is an example of professional consensus-building and nationwide participation. The Council recommends that national education standards build upon the following current professional efforts.

English

Literature is the subject matter specific to the English curriculum. Reading and writing, speaking and listening are communication skills that underlie it. The content and processes of the English curriculum enrich life experiences, increase employability, and enhance communication. Standards developed in this subject have broad applicability in every subject of the curriculum.

All students, regardless of background, should have access to both the content and processes of the English curriculum and be able to respond thoughtfully and knowledgeably about a wide variety of major works of high-quality literature. Students sometimes have not been introduced to literature because the focus has been on the basic skills. Often, writing is little more than filling in the blanks or composing a single sentence.

Important work has been done in this area by a number of states and organizations. For example, the assessment frameworks for reading and writing created by the National Assessment Governing Board for the National Assessment of Educational Progress (NAEP) and the curriculum guidelines created by the state of Maine may be useful to examine in any standards-setting effort.

Mathematics

All students need a solid foundation in mathematics that goes beyond simple arithmetic and includes analytical and problem-solving operations. Of all the subject areas, mathematics is now the one in which the United States is farthest along in the standards-setting process. The National Council of Teachers of Mathematics has developed curriculum standards through an extensive iterative process with broad public input and professional review that has resulted in unprecedented consensus. These are gaining wide acceptance in education and in the public arena as a framework for the mathematics that schools should teach.

Defining standards for levels of student mathematics performance — what knowledge and skills students should master — still remains to be done. That process should build upon the important work under way in many states and countries.

Science

Given the fast pace of technological development, all students need a firm grasp of the concepts and thinking skills involved in science. Students can learn information about the world around them in a manner that also teaches them to reason and investigate scientifically.

With the support of the U.S. Department of Education, the National Academy of Sciences has recently started a major effort to develop world-class standards for what students should know

Science For All Students

- World norms for what constitutes a basic education have changed radically in response to the rapid growth of scientific knowledge and technological power.
- Sweeping changes in the entire educational system from kindergarten through twelfth grade will have to be made if the United States is to become a nation of scientifically literate citizens.
- A necessary first step in achieving systematic reform in science, mathematics, and technology education is reaching a clear understanding of what constitutes scientific literacy.

Excerpted from: Science For All Americans: A Project 2061 Report On Literacy Goals in Science, Mathematics, and Technology, *American Association for the Advancement of Science. (1989).*

and be able to do in science. Such promising work as that of *Project 2061* of the American Association for the Advancement of Science (AAAS), the NAEP science framework, the National Science Teachers Association's *Scope, Sequence and Coordination* projects, and several state science frameworks will form the basis of the consensus-building activity to be conducted by the National Academy of Sciences.

History

Understanding the past provides a context for understanding the present. The study of history is more than a superficial recognition of names and dates. It involves indepth knowledge of the important people, ideas, events, and trends that have helped to shape the world. In addition to major political events, history includes such areas as social and economic developments over time, civics, art and music, and the history of ideas. The links between history and geography should be explicit and should demonstrate the roots of events in time and place. Knowledge of the history of other nations and their cultures broadens students' perspectives. A solid grasp of America's history teaches students an appreciation for both the diversity and the shared experiences and values that have given the United States its unique character.

Given the size and diversity of the country, it is difficult to craft a plan for history education that balances pluralism and common values. In California, a state with a very diverse population, the *History-Social Science Framework* has been widely acclaimed for scholarly integrity and multicultural perspective. The National Center for History in the Schools at UCLA has embarked on a two-year effort to develop world-class history standards with support from the National Endowment for the Humanities and the U.S. Department of Education.

Geography

Educated citizens need to understand their geographic setting in the world and that of other peoples. Geography, understood broadly, includes historical, political, social, economic, and physical interaction with the Earth and its environment.

What we now expect our students to know in geography is minimal when compared to what other developed nations expect of their students in this subject. There is substantial concern about the negative consequences this may have for our ability to market American goods and services in different parts of the world.

World-class standards should be developed in geography, broadly defined. The leadership of the National Geographic Society has provided impetus for work on setting guidelines, designing new materials, and providing professional development opportunities for teachers. The *Guidelines for Geographic Education*, developed by the National Council for Geographic Education and the Association of American Geographers, would be worth examining in the course of setting standards for this subject.

Geography is Vital

Americans' ignorance of their own country and of the world will have dire consequences for our nation's welfare, strength, and global interdependence and for the effects we have on people in other nations. Our very livelihoods depend upon products, ideas, and even weather and climate that originate great distances from where we live and work. In a democracy the development of compassionate and effective public policies depends upon active participation of citizens who are broadly educated about their own society and its relations with the entire world. All events affecting society occur within a geographic context. To understand these events fully we must subject them to geographic scrutiny.

Excerpted from: Guidelines for Geographic Education: Elementary and Secondary Schools., *Joint Committee on Geographic Education of the National Council for Geographic Education and the Association of American Geographers. (1984).*

Toward a System of Assessing the National Standards

To make national standards meaningful, it is important that the Nation be able to measure progress toward them. The Council recommends a system of multiple assessments linked to the national standards that will measure the progress of individuals, schools, districts, states, and the Nation.

The system of assessments would have two major components: individual student assessments and assessments of representative samples of students from which inferences about the quality of programs or educational systems could be made. The National Assessment of Educational Progress (NAEP) is an example of a large-scale sample assessment. Both components would be aligned with the national standards.

Purposes of Assessment

In endorsing assessments to monitor individual and system progress toward the national education standards, the Council is advocating a system that will provide information for the following purposes:

- to exemplify for students, parents, and teachers the kinds and levels of achievement that should be expected;

- to improve classroom instruction and improve the learning outcomes for all students;

- to inform students, parents, and teachers about student progress toward the standards;

- to measure and hold students, schools, districts, states, and the Nation accountable for educational performance; and

- to assist in education program decisions to be made by policy makers.

The Council notes that it is unlikely that all of these purposes can be accomplished with the same test or assessment instrument.

Individual Student Assessments

New student assessments will need to be developed by states, districts, commercial publishers, and others in order to measure student performance against the national content and performance standards. To facilitate the sound development of such new assessments, the Council recommends the following:

- New student assessments should incorporate the best thinking and sound research and development.

- States should work together in developing assessment instruments in order to use resources effectively and to improve the quality of the assessments.

- States and others should examine various approaches in designing student assessments of the national standards and also develop innovative methods of administration and improved procedures to report to their multiple audiences.

- Different assessments may be developed for different curricula. There will be diverse interpretations of the content standards that lead to differing curricula and teaching practices.

- High stakes should not be associated with the results of any assessment until the qualities of validity, reliability, and fairness have been addressed.

The Council finds, however, that the assessments eventually could be used for such high-stakes purposes for students as high school graduation, college admission, continuing education, or certification for employment. Assessments could also be used by states and localities as the basis for system accountability.

Assessments of Samples of Students

The Council recommends that the National Assessment of Educational Progress (NAEP) be reauthorized and assured funding to monitor the Nation's and states' progress toward Goals 3 and 4 of the National Education Goals. NAEP is the national program begun in 1969 to biannually test representative samples of students in grades 4, 8, and 12 in core subject areas and report achievement trends over time. As national standards are developed, there should be efforts to ensure that NAEP will be aligned with these standards.

Technical Issues Associated with Improving Assessments

Currently, a substantial amount of testing is conducted in schools. It is frequently said that American students are tested more than others in the world. Despite all the tests, surprisingly little useful information is available to students, parents, educators, and policymakers. Dissatisfaction with shortcomings in present practices has led to a rich variety of efforts to improve assessments. A national effort is needed to facilitate and coordinate these activities.

The new assessments should challenge all students and educators to do their best, open up new opportunities for students, and provide real incentives to improve the quality of America's schools. There is significant interest in the promise of performance-based assessments, such as portfolios and projects, as ways of collecting evidence of what students know and can do. Such assessments frequently use open-ended tasks, focus on higher order or complex thinking skills, require significant student time, and may allow students to choose among alternative tasks; some examine the performance of group activities. While important issues remain to be resolved, innovative techniques used by states and localities may be important elements in the mix of assessment instruments that will make up the new national system.

Important technical difficulties confront those developing such a new system of assessments. The Council deliberated on these complexities and recommends that special precautions be taken in the development process. First, any system must honor the traditions of local and state responsibility for education and,

Grading the Advanced Placement Examination

Advanced Placement grading procedures were developed with certain features intended to ensure high score reliability. There is a "Chief Reader" who has primary responsibility for the grading in each subject. In consultation with the test development committee, the Chief Reader creates a tentative set of standards by which the answers are to be judged. The Chief Reader oversees all the other "Readers" in that subject. In most subjects, the Chief Reader receives help in assigning grades from those who designed the questions and others so as to ensure that the standards are being applied consistently. Readers are trained by grading "samples" — copies of actual answers distributed among all Readers of the same section of the exam.

The reading and scoring of "live" papers does not begin until consistency has been achieved in the grading of the samples. Throughout the grading, samples are used daily at frequent intervals to ensure that the scoring remains uniform. A constant check of random papers from each Reader is made to further ensure consistent application of the standards. Grading reliability studies are conducted for all examinations.

The final grade on an examination is the composite of the score on the multiple-choice section plus the scores given by the Readers, weighted and combined. Using guidelines established for this purpose, the total composite score is translated by the Chief Reader into the scale used for reporting the grades: 1 through 5 (5 = extremely well qualified; 4 = well qualified; 3 = qualified; 2 = possibly qualified; 1 = no recommendation).

Summarized from: School Administrator's Guide to the Advanced Placement Program. *The Advanced Placement Program. The College Board. (Edition H).*

---

consequently, must provide flexibility and room for local adaptation. Second, there are difficulties in producing assessments of high technical quality and fairness. Third, acknowledging that an assessment system of the scope imagined is a new enterprise for the Nation, care must be taken to avoid the unintended and undesired effects of some testing practices, such as narrowing instruction and excluding certain students from assessments. Sufficient safeguards must be built into the system to protect students from negative consequences while the system of assessments is being refined, especially for students who have not been well served by testing in the past.

It will be technically difficult but essential to ensure that new assessments are valid, reliable, and fair. This requires ongoing reviews of the emerging assessments and their uses. Further, particularly for children who have historically experienced less success in school — such as the poor, ethnic minorities, and students with disabilities — opportunity to learn is a critical condition for valid and fair use of assessment results.

First-Rate System of Assessments

The development of a first-rate system of assessments will be an evolutionary, ongoing process. The Council finds the following activities to be crucial in this effort:

- *Quality assurance.* The Council recommends a quality assurance process to ensure that new student assessments are appropriate measures of the national standards and meet the technical considerations of validity, reliability, and fairness, particularly in conjunction with any high-stakes uses. Judgments of validity, reliability, and fairness depend in part upon how the results of the assessments are used.

- *Quality guidelines for assessment development.* The Council recommends quality guidelines for the development and use of student assessments such as the *Standards for Educational and Psychological Testing* and the criteria described by the National Forum on Assessment. Revised and additional guidelines may be needed as work progresses.

- *Comparability.* The Council finds it essential that different assessments produce comparable results in attainment of the standards.

- *Coherent and informative results.* One key objective of the assessment effort is to provide accurate information for students, parents, and teachers about the educational progress of individual students; another is to inform the public about the national achievement level. For students, parents, and teachers, the national system of assessments should provide information about an individual student's performance against national standards. States and localities should report results in the context of the conditions of learning and students' opportunities to learn.

- *Independent reviews.* The Council recommends periodic, independent reviews of the assessment system to examine its impact, to ensure alignment with the national standards, and to ensure comparability of results.

- *Better knowledge base.* The Council recommends continued research on developing, interpreting, and reporting assessments and ensuring test comparability.

- *Cost effectiveness.* Detailed cost estimates for a new system of assessments are not available, but the Council recommends that assessments be cost effective. They should seek to build on current efforts at the state and local levels. The Council does not intend that the assessment system add to the net burden of testing, but rather that much current testing be replaced.

The Council finds precedents which indicate setting high standards and developing a quality system of assessments can raise student achievement. The Council advocates moving ahead to create high national standards and a voluntary system of assessments with careful and ongoing oversight of the process and its results.

Raising Standards for American Education

How Are National Standards and a System of Assessments to be Developed and Implemented?

The Council recommends that a coordinating structure be put in place to advance standards-setting and assessment development. Development and implementation of national standards and a system of assessments should not take place in isolation but should be part of comprehensive educational reform. Indeed, the intellectual and political activities of setting high national standards and developing assessments are likely to provide added momentum for higher expectations and educational renewal.

Proposed Coordinating Structure

The Council has agreed that the Nation should move forward to set national education standards and develop a voluntary national system of assessments to help students and schools meet those standards. To ensure that this is done effectively, a coordinating structure needs to be agreed upon and put into place.

Principles

- *Non-Federal.* To maintain the Nation's tradition of state and local authority over education, any new oversight entity should be part of a cooperative national effort.

- *Non-Duplication.* The process should benefit from and not attempt to duplicate work being done by existing entities.

- *Broad-Based.* The coordinating structure should be bipartisan, engage government at all levels, and involve the many constituencies that have an interest in improving education.

- *Accountability.* The coordinating structure must nevertheless be accountable to the public. In addition to a public appointment process, appropriate constraints on rules of deliberation, reporting, and contracting can help provide such accountability.

- *Timing.* Much good work has already begun and much more needs to be done soon. The coordinating structure should be in place quickly and act as a catalyst for progress rather than retard current efforts.

Functions

A number of functions need to be performed to achieve the development of standards and assessments. They are described as follows:

Standards

- Coordinate the development of national standards
- Develop an overarching statement
- Develop content standards
- Develop student performance standards
- Develop school delivery standards
- Develop system performance standards
- Certify content and student performance standards as world class

Assessments

- Coordinate the development of a system of assessments for individual students consistent with the national standards
- Develop a program/system monitor consistent with national standards

- Provide research and development for break-the-mold assessments
- Issue guidelines for assessments
- Ensure technical merit (validity, reliability, fairness)
- Certify assessments
- Establish procedures and criteria for achieving comparability

Structure

The National Education Goals Panel would be reconfigured to be politically balanced. Representation would include two members from the Administration; eight Governors with three from the same political party as the President appointed by the chair or vice chair of the National Governors' Association, whichever represents the same political party, in consultation with each other; four members of Congress appointed by the majority and minority leaders of the U.S. Senate and U.S. House of Representatives. The role and function of the Panel would remain the same as set out in its charter. In addition, it will appoint members to a newly created body called the National Education Standards and Assessments Council, and it will certify standards and criteria for assessments.

Work on several of the functions identified above has already begun. For instance, professional groups in the five disciplines are developing national content standards with financial support from the U.S. Department of Education's Office of Educational Research and Improvement, the National Endowment for the Humanities,National Science Foundation, and other existing federal and non-federal agencies. The National Assessment of Educational Progress, with oversight by the National Assessment Governing Board, is developing assessments which would function as the program/system monitor; and the federal government is funding through the Office of Educational Research and Improvement important research and development for break-the-mold assessments. This work would continue and in fact would need to be augmented and accelerated. Other work, such as the school and system standards, would be developed by states working collectively through organizations like the National Governors' Association, the Education Commission of the States, the Council of Chief State School Officers, and state legislative organizations.

Nevertheless, a coordinating body is still needed to ensure the establishment of national education standards and a system of assessments. This body would be a catalyst and provide oversight and leadership. The body would establish guidelines for standards-setting and assessment development and general criteria to determine the appropriateness of standards and assessments recommended. This body would be the National Education Standards and Assessments Council (NESAC).

It is vital that there be strong public accountability in this work. For this reason, NESAC would be appointed by the Panel. Certification of content and student performance standards and criteria for assessments as world class shall be the joint responsibility of the Panel and NESAC. No certification will be issued by the Panel except after approval of NESAC and in the event the Panel denies certification to all or part of a NESAC proposal, all or part of that proposal shall be returned to NESAC with the reasons for denial.

It is desirable that Congress and the President codify the reconstituted Goals Panel and the National Education Standards and Assessments Council, consistent with the Panel's charter and this coordinating structure, and appropriate line-item funds for their operation to be administered through the U.S. Department of Education. However, the Goals Panel and NESAC would be allowed substantial latitude in their operation and would be as independent of the U.S. Congress, the U.S. Department of Education, and other federal agencies as permissible under federal law. The Panel and NESAC will each be able to hire staff, enter into contracts, make grants, receive funds both private and public, form committees, hire consultants and have gift authority.

To the extent practicable, the characteristic of these entities as voluntary partnerships committed to transforming American education by encouraging the Nation to strive for and achieve the National Education Goals and World Class Standards would be maintained.

Membership

NESAC would consist of 21 members to include one-third public officials, one-third educators, and one-third members of the general public including consumers of education. The members would be appointed for three-year terms, with no individual serving more than six consecutive years. Officers would be elected for one-year terms. No person can serve on both the Goals Panel and NESAC.

Because NESAC will be making determinations and recommendations on the merit of standards and assessments, the appointment process must take potential conflict-of-interest considerations into careful account.

Appointment Process

Nominations for positions on NESAC would be sought from the general public and from these nominations the Panel would make appointments according to the established categories. The Panel would establish initial terms for individuals of two, three, or four years in order to establish a rotation in which one-third of the members are selected each year.

As vacancies arise on NESAC, the Panel would seek nominations from the general public and the Panel would make the appropriate appointments.

National Standards and a System of Assessments as Parts of Comprehensive Educational Reform

Structures and processes not only have to be put in place to develop standards and assessments but are also needed to support their use by schools throughout the Nation. Sound programs of instruction must be tied to standards and assessments. The Council recognizes that states, local communities, and schools set important policies that establish the context in which standards and assessments will operate. These include policies and practices regarding curriculum, professional development, school restructuring, and community and family supports. Such reforms should not be piecemeal. To be most effective, they must operate in an integrated fashion.

Comprehensive systemic reform should affect all elements of the education system. Families, educators, and policymakers must all work together. Their efforts at the school, district, state, and national levels should address four major dimensions of educational renewal: reforming schools, engaging families and communities, creating incentives for high performance, and providing equitable opportunities to achieve the new standards.

Reforming Schools

All children must have the opportunity to learn the material that new standards will indicate they should know. Improved instructional materials and instruction based on the standards are essential. Schools will need curriculum frameworks oriented to high levels of performance that are based on the national education standards.

New assessments should be designed to guide instruction and learning. What is expected should be clear enough that teachers can prepare students for the assessments and teachers should be able to use the results to revise and improve their teaching. Teachers must be active participants in the design of curricula and assessments tied to the standards.

High standards of achievement for all students will have implications for how America prepares, licenses, and certifies its teachers. To teach successfully to the new standards, teachers will need a deeper knowledge of subject matter and a better understanding of pedagogy. Substantial cooperation from universities, especially colleges of arts and sciences, in teacher preparation will be required. The National Board for Professional Teaching Standards has embarked on an effort to set national, voluntary standards for experienced teachers that would promote quality instructional practices.

A comprehensive inservice professional development initiative is also essential in preparing teachers to help students attain the national education standards. States have a critical role in helping to make the most successful practices in professional development accessible to all personnel. Professional development must also be available to school and district administrators, who play key leadership roles in school reform.

Schools, school districts, and states should be encouraged to experiment with alternative strategies to help students achieve the new standards. New roles and responsibilities are likely to be necessary for success. Reforms that seek to make educators accountable also need to provide them with commensurate authority.

Education technology holds promise for helping students and schools achieve the standards and will be a basic requirement for education in the 21st century. Possibilities include distance learning that permits greater access for teachers and students to courses offered in different locations, and computer and video technologies for the delivery of enriched interactive learning. Teachers and principals in all schools will need professional development in educational technology. New technologies aligned to the standards and system of assessments may be included among the curriculum resources designed to achieve the standards.

Engaging Families and Communities

The conditions of childhood are changing and some of the most significant changes have to do with characteristics of families. Helping families so that they may help students attain the high standards will require new strategies for coordinating the efforts of home and school.

Communities create the context in which schools and families function. Concerned communities value learning and provide necessary support to families so that learning can thrive. An important community service that is also supported by state and federal government is to provide the early childhood programs that help prepare children for school. The National Education Goals set objectives relating to nutrition and health care, access to preschools, and parent education. Programs have begun at the national, state, and local levels to foster coordination of family health care and social services.

National standards can clarify what a community can expect of its schools and help define a need for public action. Too frequently school reforms fall short of expectations because members of the public do not understand how they can play a constructive role in improving their schools. Efforts are needed to enhance local awareness of the need for change and to create shared understandings of educational problems and potential solutions.

Creating Incentives for High Performance

Meeting high standards will entail comprehensive change, and the students, families, educators, and communities involved will need to have a reason to change. Currently, incentives for students and educators are overly focused on compliance with rules and regulations. They should be focused on attaining high performance. While intrinsic rewards such as love of learning are the best — and often primary — motivation, it is clear that external factors also play an important role in how hard both students and educators work. Rewards for success and constructive intervention in cases of persistent failure may be tied to student outcomes for both students and educators. Since learning requires the active participation of both, it would be unfair to focus incentives only on one or the other. Today, students not applying to highly selective colleges often fail to see a reason to enroll in demanding high school courses and to do their best. All students should be provided incentives for meeting world-class standards. Incentives for educators should focus on improvement, including success in educating those students who have been least well served in the past.

Ensuring Equity

Providing genuine opportunity for all students to achieve high standards is a national moral imperative. The standards that the Council proposes would apply to the entire education system. All students must have the opportunity to achieve them and to be assessed fairly on their attainment. To bring this about, equitable educational opportunities must be provided.

The Council recognizes the concerns of those who are fearful of the unintended consequences of its proposals. Yet high standards and knowledge gained from appropriate assessments could serve as rallying points to secure the school and community efforts needed to reach them. High-quality standards and assessments should mobilize educators and the public to reform schools, engage families and communities, create incentives for high performance, and provide genuine opportunity for all students.

Raising Standards for American Education

The National Education Goals Panel has called upon America to become a nation of learners. National standards and assessments linked to them, developed through a broad consensus process, are a critical next step in revitalizing American education. To succeed, standards and assessments must be part of a fundamental reform of schools and school systems.

The move toward high standards will require mobilizing the entire country. Families, communities, schools, educators, employers, policymakers, and students have important roles to play in the comprehensive effort to fashion new standards and to see that they are attained.

The goal is ambitious and the stakes are high. Raising standards can transform what is taught and how instruction takes place. Raising standards can change the view of responsibilities in education.Raising standards can improve the quality of performance, not just in the classroom but on the job, in the marketplace, and in all aspects of American life.

Raising Standards for American Education

Appendices

Acknowledgements

This report was prepared by the National Council on Education Standards and Testing. The work of the Council was supported by reports from eight task forces and expert testimony. In this process, many individuals gave generously of their time, experience, and knowledge. The Council wishes to thank all those listed in this appendix.

The Council wishes to thank its staff for their extraordinary efforts in assisting the Council in its work and in the preparation of this report.

Staff of the National Council on Education Standards and Testing

Francie Alexander
Executive Director

David L. Stevenson
Deputy Executive Director

Lawrence Feinberg
Policy Development Associate

Theodor Rebarber
Research Associate

Emily O. Wurtz
Senior Education Associate

Liz Barnes
Program Analyst

Ron Myers
Executive Assistant

Charles J. Walter
Executive Officer

Amy Leigh Hatfield
Program Assistant

Linda E. Martin
Consultant

Paula A. Shipp
Program Assistant

Michael F. Smith
Program Assistant

Nancy Delasos
Office Assistant

G. Monique Waddell
Secretary

The staff received editing and technical assistance from the following individuals:

Carter Nicely   C. Claire Smith   Joyce D. Stern

Task Force Members

Eight task forces were created, each to advise the National Council on a specific discipline or an aspect of standards, testing, and assessment. The eight task forces focused on the topics Standards, Assessment, Implementation, English, Mathematics, Science, History, and Geography. Each task force was chaired by a member of the National Council and included additional Council members as well as other experts and representatives of concerned organizations. The Task Force Membership follows:

Standards Task Force

Marshall S. Smith
Task Force Chair and Council member, Stanford University, Stanford, California

Gordon Ambach
Council member, Council of Chief State School Officers, Washington, D.C.

Brian L. Benzel
Council member, Edmonds School District, Lynnwood, Washington

Chester E. Finn, Jr.,
Council member, Vanderbilt University, Washington,D.C.

Lauren Resnick
Council member, University of Pittsburgh, Pittsburgh, Pennsylvania

John Anderson
IBM, Washington,D.C.

Ernest Boyer
The Carnegie Foundation for the Advancement of Teaching, Princeton, New Jersey

William Demmert
Stanford University, Stanford, California

Marian Wright Edelman and Denise Alston
Children's Defense Fund, Washington,D.C.

Susan Fuhrman
Rutgers University, New Brunswick, New Jersey

Janis Gabay
Junipero Serra High School, San Diego, California

Jack Harr
ABC Inc., New York, New York

Bill Honig
California State Department of Education, Sacramento, California

Barbara S. Nielsen
South Carolina State Department of Education, Columbia, South Carolina

Conrad Snowden
D.C. Committee on Public Education, Washington,D.C.

Roberto Zamora
La Joya Independent School District, La Joya, Texas

Assessment Task Force

Eva L. Baker
Task Force Chair and Council member, U.C.L.A., Los Angeles, California

David Kearns
Council member, U.S. Department of Education, Washington, D.C.

Edward L. Meyen
Council member, University of Kansas, Lawrence, Kansas

Joan Baron
Connecticut State Department of Education, Hartford, Connecticut

Curtis Banks
Howard University, Washington, D.C.

Dale Carlson
California State Department of Education, Sacramento, California

Georgia Earnest Garcia
University of Illinois, Urbana-Champaign, Illinois

Edmund Gordon
Yale University, New Haven, Connecticut

Dan Koretz
RAND, Washington, D.C.

Kenji Hakuta
Stanford University, Stanford, California

Robert L. Linn
University of Colorado, Boulder, Colorado

George Madaus
Boston College, Chestnut Hill, Massachusetts

Eduardo Rodriguez
Mesquite, New Mexico

Luther W. Seabrook
South Carolina State Department of Education, Columbia, South Carolina

Sheila Valencia
University of Washington, Seattle, Washington

Dennie Wolf
Harvard University, Cambridge, Massachusetts

Implementation Task Force

David Hornbeck
Task Force Chair and Council member, David W. Hornbeck and Associates, Baltimore, Maryland

Jeff Bingaman
Council member, United States Senate, New Mexico

Michael Nettles
Council member, University of Tennessee, Knoxville, Tennessee

Roger Semerad
Council member, RJR Nabisco, Inc., Washington, D.C.

Albert Shanker
Council member, American Federation of Teachers, Washington, D.C.

Betty Castor
Florida State Department of Education, Tallahassee, Florida

Henry Cauthen
ETV Commission, Columbia, South Carolina

Dan Chernow
Pacific Theatres Corp., Los Angeles, California

David Cohen
Michigan State University, East Lansing, Michigan

Waylon Edwards
Laramie County School District, Cheyenne, Wyoming

Sonia C. Hernandez
Office of the Governor, Austin, Texas

Miguel Ley
Ross Elementary School, Washington, D.C.

Dotty Luebke
Eastman Kodak, Rochester, New York

Phillip Schlecty
Professional Development Center, Louisville, Kentucky

Lee S. Shulman
Stanford University, Stanford, California

Jim Steyer
Children Now, Oakland, California

Jonathan Wilson
Law Firm of Davis, Hockenberg, Des Moines, Iowa

English Task Force

Martha Fricke
Task Force Chair and Council member, Ashland School Board, Ashland, Nebraska

Mary Curtiss
Trumbull High School, Trumbull, Connecticut

Kristina Elias
Greenwich Public Schools, Greenwich, Connecticut

Janice Haynes
CIMS/CA, Bronx, New York

Barbara Kapinus
Maryland State Department of Education, Hyattsville, Maryland

Leanna Landsmann
Landsmann & Schutz, New York, New York

Judith Langer
State University of New York, Albany, New York

Anita Moss
University of North Carolina, Charlotte, North Carolina

P. David Pearson
University of Illinois at Urbana-Champaign, Illinois

Fran Perkins
University of Alabama, Birmingham, Alabama

Winifred M. Radigan
Brooklyn High Schools Office, Brooklyn, New York

Barbara Schmidt
California State University, Sacramento, California

Mathematics Task Force

Iris Carl
Task Force Chair and Council member, National Council of Teachers of Mathematics, Houston, Texas

Gail Burrill
Whitnall High School, Greenfield, Wisconsin

Arnold Cutler
Mounds View High School, St. Paul, Minnesota

Wesley Day
Norwalk High School, Norwalk, Iowa

Walter Denham
*California State Department of Education, Sacramento,
California*

John Dossey
Illinois State University, Normal, Illinois

Paula Duckett
*River Terrace Community Elementary School, Washington,
D.C.*

Shirley Hill
University of Missouri, Kansas City, Missouri

Jeremy Kilpatrick
University of Georgia, Athens, Georgia

Tej Pandey
*California State Department of Education, Sacramento,
California*

Dorothy Strong
Chicago Public Schools, Chicago, Illinois

Science Task Force

Mark Musick
*Task Force Chair and Council member, Southern Regional
Education Board, Atlanta, Georgia*

Eve M. Bither
*Council member, Maine State Department of Education,
Augusta, Maine*

Carlos Cisneros
Council member, New Mexico State Senate, Questa, New Mexico

Walter Massey
*Council member, National Science Foundation, Washington,-
D.C.*

Erma Anderson
Congressional Fellow, Needmore, Pennsylvania

Mary Budd Rowe
Stanford University, Stanford, California

Thomas Cech
University of Colorado, Boulder, Colorado

Audrey Champagne
State University of New York, Albany, New York

Fielding Gentry
Sousa Junior High School, Washington, D.C.

Charles R. Hogen
The Merck Company Foundation, New Jersey

Maria Lopez-Freeman
Achievement Council, Los Angeles, California
James Minstrell
Mercer Island High School, Mercer Island, Washington
Jerry Pine
California Institute of Technology, Pasadena, California
Senta Raizen
National Center for Improving Science Education, Washington, D.C.

History Task Force
Lynne V. Cheney
Task Force Chair and Council member, National Endowment for the Humanities, Washington, D.C.
Mary Bicouvaris
Council member, Hampton Roads Academy, Newport News, Virginia
John Hainkel
Council member, Louisiana State Senate, Baton Rouge, Louisiana
Samuel L. Banks
Baltimore City Public Schools, Baltimore, Maryland
Jim Breedlove
BellSouth, Atlanta, Georgia
Hank Cotton
Cherry Creek Schools (retired), Englewood, Colorado
Charlotte Crabtree
U.C.L.A., Los Angeles, California
Claudia Hoone
Ralph Waldo Emerson School, Indianapolis, Indiana
William H. McNeill
University of Chicago (retired), Chicago, Illinois
C. Frederick Risinger
Indiana University, Bloomington, Indiana
Ruben Zepeda
Grant High School, Van Nuys, California

Geography Task Force
Sally B. Pancrazio
Task Force Chair and Council member, Illinois State University, Normal, Illinois
Sandra Hassan
Council member, Beach Channel High School, Rockaway Park, New York
Norm Bettis
Illinois State University, Normal, Illinois
Richard Boehm
Southwest Texas State University, San Marcos, Texas

Muncel Chang
National Council for Geographic Education, Indiana,
Pennsylvania

Roger Downs
Pennsylvania State University, University Park, Pennsylvania

Cindy Hansen
TRW, Cleveland, Ohio

Rita Duarte Herrera
Alum Rock Union School District, San Jose, California

Corine O'Donnell
Campbell Elementary, Arvada, Colorado

Kit Salter
University of Missouri, Columbia, Missouri

Terry Smith
National Geographic Society, Washington,D.C.

Joseph Weaver
Oak Hill High School, Converse, Indiana

Tom Wilbanks
Oak Ridge National Laboratory, Oak Ridge, Tennessee

Presenters

The Council requested formal presentations from many authorities in
their areas of expertise. These presentations informed the Council on
the status and complexities of efforts to set standards and improve
assessment. Their contribution helped the work of the Council. We
wish to thank the following people who made presentations to the
Council on the dates noted:

June 24, 1991
Gordon Ambach
Council of Chief State School Officers

Eva L. Baker
CRESST, U.C.L.A.

Bonnie Brunkhorst
National Science Teachers Association

Charlotte Crabtree
National Center for History in the Schools, U.C.L.A.

Sarah Warshauer Freedman
National Center for the Study of Writing and Literacy

Edmund Gordon
Yale University

Paul Gagnon
National Council for History Education

Kenneth Hoffman
National Research Council

Mary Lindquist
National Council of Teachers of Mathematics

Gail Ludwig
National Council for Geographic Education

Miles Myers
National Council of Teachers of English

P. David Pearson
University of Illinois at Urbana-Champaign

James Rutherford
American Association for the Advancement of Science

Kit Salter
Association of American Geographers

Terry Smith
National Geographic Society

July 18, 1991

Joan Baron
Connecticut State Department of Education

Ross Brewer
Vermont State Department of Education

Jeremy Kilpatrick
University of Georgia

Magdalene Lampert
Michigan State University

Tej Pandey
California State Department of Education

Thomas Romberg
University of Wisconsin, Madison, Wisconsin

August 15, 1991

Phyllis Aldrich
National Assessment Governing Board

Pascal D. Forgione, Jr.
National Education Goals Panel

Ina Mullis
Educational Testing Service (also presented at September 23 meeting)

Claire Pelton
National Board for Professional Teaching Standards

Ramsay Selden
Council of Chief State School Officers

September 23, 1991

Tom Boysen
Kentucky State Department of Education

Dale Carlson
California State Department of Education

John Dossey
Illinois State University
Emerson Elliott
National Center for Education Statistics
Barbara Kapinus
Maryland State Department of Education
Archie Lapointe
Educational Testing Service
John Murphy
New York State Department of Education
Norma Paulus
Oregon State Department of Education

November 19, 1991
Linda Darling-Hammond
Teachers' College, Columbia University
H.D. Hoover
University of Iowa

Staff of Council Members

Critical assistance was provided by staff members of the Co-Chairs of the Council. Their help was invaluable throughout the process, from the initial meetings to the final production of the report. Special thanks goes to these individuals.

Nikki McNamee
Office of the Governor, South Carolina
Janice Trawick
Office of the Governor, South Carolina
Nancy Sanders
Office of the Governor, Colorado
B.J. Thornberry
Office of the Governor, Colorado

All members of the Council have relied on their personal staffs to handle many of the important details involved in the work of the Council. Staff members attended meetings and made suggestions and recommendations that were incorporated into the final report. We wish to thank the following individuals for their professionalism and dedication.

Lida Barrett
National Science Foundation
Laurie Chivers
Committee on Labor and Human Resources
Dotty Clark
National School Boards Association

Glen Cutlip
National Eduation Association
Emerson Elliott
National Center for Education Statistics
Pascal D. Forgione, Jr.
National Education Goals Panel
Ed Fuentes
National Education Goals Panel
Milton Goldberg
United States Department of Education
Lanny Griffith
United States Department of Education
June Harris
Committee on Education and Labor
Susan Greene
National Governors' Association
Andrew Hartman
Committee on Education and Labor
Charles Kolb
Office of Policy Development, The White House
Jack Jennings
Committee on Education and Labor
Martharose Laffey
National School Boards Association
Bruno Manno
United States Department of Education
Jerry Martin
National Endowment for the Humanities
Jeff McFarland
Subcommittee on Elementary, Secondary, and Vocational Education
Lynn Munson
National Endowment for the Humanities
Rae Nelson
Office of Policy Development, The White House
Ray Ramirez
Office of Senator Bingaman, New Mexico
Bella Rosenberg
American Federation of Teachers
Jeff Thomas
National Endowment for the Humanities
Damian Thorman
Subcommittee on Elementary, Secondary, and Vocational Education
Doreen Torgerson
Office of Policy Development, The White House

Susan Traiman
National Governors' Association

Susan Wilhelm
Subcommittee on Elementary, Secondary, and Vocational Education

Luther Williams
National Science Foundation

Special Support

We would like to express our appreciation to the following individuals and organizations who assisted us at various times during the course of our work:

- The National Geographic Society for their help in final preparation of the report; Terry Smith for coordination of the work, David Griffin for layout and design, and Mark Nardini for the cover art;
- Diane Ravitch, Assistant Secretary, Office of Educational Research and Improvement, U.S. Department of Education; Joseph Conaty, Designated Federal Official, Office of Educational Research and Improvement, U.S. Department of Education;
- Jim Breedlove, BellSouth; Gil Grosvenor, National Geographic Society; Bill Honig, California Department of Education; and Walter Massey, National Science and Technology Week Trust Fund of the National Science Foundation contributed their time and resources;
- Susan Fuhrman, Rutgers University; and Edward B. Fiske for their editorial suggestions.

Authorization for the National Council on Education Standards and Testing

Purpose

The National Council on Education Standards and Testing was created by Public Law 102-62 on June 27, 1991. The purpose of the Council is to provide advice on the desirability and feasibility of national standards and testing in education.

The Council was created in response to findings of Congress that:

- Organizations have begun developing national education standards for various subject areas and grade levels;
- Groups have called for the expansion of national testing for school children;
- Decisions regarding the desirability and feasibility of additional national testing should follow such decisions on national standards for education;
- Efforts regarding national standards and testing should be undertaken with the broadest possible participation by the public; and
- A major national council is needed to assure broad participation by the public, to provide a focus for national debate on national education standards and testing, and to provide advice on the desirability and feasibility of developing national standards and testing.

Duties

The duties of the Council shall be to advise the American people
as to —

1) Whether suitable specific education standards should and can be
   established, such as world class standards, for —
   (a) the knowledge and skills that students should possess and
       that schools should impart in order that American students
       leave grades 4, 8 and 12 demonstrating competency in
       challenging subject matter including English, mathematics,
       science, history, and geography; and
   (b) every school in America to ensure that all students learn to
       use their minds well so that they will be prepared for
       responsible citizenship, further learning, and productive
       employment in our modern economy; and
2) Whether, while respecting State and local control of education, an
   appropriate system of voluntary national tests or examinations
   should and can be established, such as American achievement
   tests, that will provide prompt, accurate information to parents,
   educators, and policy makers on the progress being made toward
   the specific education standards by individual students, schools,
   school systems, States, and the Nation as a whole (if such
   standards can be established). The goal of any such system shall
   be to foster good teaching and learning, as well to monitor
   performance.

Final Report

The Council shall, as soon as possible, but not later than December 31,
1991, submit a report to the Congress, the Secretary of Education,
and the National Education Goals Panel that contains
recommendations regarding long-term policies, structures,
mechanisms, and other important considerations with respect to the
objectives. A discussion of the validity, reliability, fairness, and costs
of implementing a system of voluntary national tests or examinations
shall also be included in such report.

Public Comment

The National Council on Education Standards and Testing has sought public comment. The comments it has received have helped to shape this report. The Council wishes to thank the individuals and organizations listed below for their suggestions and observations. The Council recognizes that while some statements submitted to it represent official positions taken by an organization, others were submitted as the views of an individual who does not claim to represent the institution with which he or she is affiliated.

- State delegations attending the National Education Forum in Des Moines, Iowa, September 27-28, 1991
- Advocates for Children of New York, Inc., Diana Autin
- Alliance for Curriculum Reform, Gordon Cawelti
- American Occupational Therapy Association, Barbara Chandler
- American Psychological Association, Wayne Camara and Gerald Sroufe
- APPLE Corps, Sallie Weddell
- Arizona State University, Carole Edelsky
- Arkansas, Office of the Governor, Deborah Walz
- Association of American Publishers, Test Committee, Michael H. Kean
- Association of Black Psychologists, Sandra Cox and Harold Dent
- Association of California School Administrators, Melinda Melendez

- Association for Supervision and Curriculum Development position statements by the national organization, state affiliates, and individual members
- Autism Society of American, David Holmes
- Brain-Based Education Network, Leslie Hart
- Brigham Young University, Utah, Rulon Garfield
- Business Roundtable and National Alliance of Business, Fritz Edelstein
- Campaign for Genuine Accountability in Education, Monty Neill
- Canton City Schools, Ohio, Wayne Denny
- Central Park East Secondary School, New York, Deborah Meier
- College Board, Donald Stewart
- Consortium for Citizens with Disabilities
- Council for Exceptional Children, Joseph Ballard and Mary Cohen
- District of Columbia, Janette Hoston Harris
- Easton Public Schools, Massachusetts, Isa Kaftal Zimmerman
- Elmbrook School District, Wisconsin, Ronald Lange
- Foxfire Teacher Outreach, Hilton Smith
- Ilima Intermediate School, Hawaii, Amy Uyechi
- Indiana University, Leonard C. Burrello
- Kamehameha Elementary School, Hawaii, Kahele Kukea
- Mariemont City Schools, Ohio, Donald Thompson
- Mexican American Legal Defense Fund, Stephen Carbo
- Midland Public School, Michigan, Carol Feider
- Mississippi Bend Area Education Agency, Richard Hanzelka
- National Alliance of Business
- NAACP Legal Defense and Education Fund, Julius Chambers
- National Center on Education Outcomes
- National Coalition of Education Activists, Debi Duke
- National Conference of State Legislatures, Education and Job Training Committee
- National Council for the Social Studies, Charlotte Anderson
- New York City Board of Ed. (District 1), Susan Harman
- Norfolk Public Schools, Virginia, George Raiss
- North Carolina, Office of the Governor, Jackie Womble Jenkins
- Northwest Association of Schools and Colleges, David Steadman
- Panasonic Foundation, Sophie Sa
- Parkway School District, Missouri, William Franzen
- Pennsylvania Department of Education, Joseph Bard
- Portage County Board of Education, Ohio, Helen Gless
- Punahou School, Hawaii, Duane Yee and Elaine Blitman
- Southern Association on Children Under Six, Cathy Grace
- Southern Regional Council, Marcia Klenbort

- Student Advocacy Center, Ruth Zweifler
- Teachers and Parents for School Renewal, Oregon, Bill Resnick
- University of California, San Diego, Tracy Strong
- Urban Superintendents' Network (Office of Educational Research and Improvement, U.S. Department of Education)

The Council also thanks the following organizations for their help in requesting public comment:

- Association for Supervision and Curriculum Development
- Business Roundtable
- Fairtest
- National Alliance of Business
- National Association of State Boards of Education
- National Conference of State Legislatures
- National Governors' Association
- National Association of School Boards

Raising Standards for American Education

The National Education Goals

Goal 1: Readiness For School

By the year 2000, all children in America will start school ready to learn.

Objectives:

- All disadvantaged and disabled children will have access to high quality and developmentally appropriate preschool programs that help prepare children for school.

- Every parent in America will be a child's first teacher and devote time each day helping his or her preschool child learn; parents will have access to the training and support they need.

- Children will receive the nutrition and health care needed to arrive at school with healthy minds and bodies, and the number of low birthweight babies will be significantly reduced through enhanced prenatal health systems.

Goal 2: High School Completion

By the year 2000, the high school graduation rate will increase to at least 90 percent.

Objectives:

- The nation must dramatically reduce its dropout rate, and seventy-five percent of those students who do drop out will successfully complete a high school degree or its equivalent.

- The gap in high school graduation rates between American students from minority backgrounds and their non-minority counterparts will be eliminated.

Goal 3: Student Achievement and Citizenship

By the year 2000, American students will leave grades four, eight, and twelve having demonstrated competency in challenging subject matter including English, mathematics, science, history, and geography; and every school in America will ensure that all students learn to use their minds well, so they may be prepared for responsible citizenship, further learning, and productive employment in our modern economy.

Objectives:

- The academic performance of elementary and secondary students will increase significantly in every quartile, and the distribution of minority students in each level will more closely reflect the student population as a whole.

- The percentage of students who demonstrate the ability to reason, solve problems, apply knowledge, and write and communicate effectively will increase substantially.

- All students will be involved in activities that promote and demonstrate good citizenship, community service, and personal responsibility.

- The percentage of students who are competent in more than one language will substantially increase.

- All students will be knowledgeable about the diverse cultural heritage of this nation and about the world community.

Goal 4: Science and Mathematics

By the year 2000, U.S. students will be first in the world in science and mathematics achievement.

Objectives:

- Math and science education will be strengthened throughout the system, especially in the early grades.

- The number of teachers with a substantive background in mathematics and science will increase by 50 percent.

- The number of U.S. undergraduate and graduate students, especially women and minorities, who complete degrees in mathematics, science, and engineering will increase significantly.

Goal 5: Adult Literacy and Lifelong Learning

By the year 2000, every adult American will be literate and will possess the knowledge and skills necessary to compete in a global economy and exercise the rights and responsibilities of citizenship.

Objectives:

- Every major American business will be involved in strengthening the connection between education and work.

- All workers will have the opportunity to acquire the knowledge and skills, from basic to highly technical, needed to adapt to emerging new technologies, work methods, and markets through public and private educational, vocational, technical, workplace, or other programs.

- The number of high-quality programs, including those at libraries, that are designed to serve more effectively the needs of the growing number of part-time and mid-career students will increase substantially.

- The proportion of those qualified students (especially minorities) who enter college, who complete at least two years, and who complete their degree programs will increase substantially.

- The proportion of college graduates who demonstrate an advanced ability to think critically, communicate effectively, and solve problems will increase substantially.

Goal 6: Safe, Disciplined and Drug-free Schools

By the year 2000, every school in America will be free of drugs and violence and will offer a disciplined environment conducive to learning.

Objectives:

- Every school will implement a firm and fair policy on use, possession, and distribution of drugs and alcohol.

- Parents, businesses, and community organizations will work together to ensure that schools are a safe haven for all children.

- Every school district will develop a comprehensive K-12 drug and alcohol prevention education program. Drug and alcohol curriculum should be taught as an integral part of health education. In addition, community-based teams should be organized to provide students and teachers with needed support.

The National Education Goals Panel was formed to report annually on the progress of the Nation and the states toward achieving the National Education Goals. Its first chair was Governor Roy Romer of Colorado, who was succeeded in August 1991 by Governor Carroll Campbell of South Carolina. The Goals Panel was originally composed of six governors, three Democrats and three Republicans; four members of the President's Administration; and four ex officio members, the majority and minority leaders of the U.S. Senate and the U.S. House of Representatives. Its first report, the *National Education Goals Report: Building a Nation of Learners*, was issued September 30, 1991.

Report of the Standards Task Force[1]

Introduction

This report responds to issues pertaining to the desirability and feasibility of national education standards posed in the legislative and supporting language of HR 2435, the enabling legislation for the National Council on Education Standards and Testing. The report specifically addresses questions raised in House Committee Report 102-104, which accompanies the enabling legislation. This introductory section of the report reviews the pertinent legislation and supporting language concerning the desirability and feasibility of national education standards, provides a brief description of the three other parts of the report, and highlights three important underlying assumptions of our work.

---

1. A draft of this report was prepared for the consideration of the National Council on Education Standards and Testing at their October, November, and December, 1991 meetings. The report was prepared by Marshall S. Smith, aided by Susan Fuhrman and Jennifer O'Day. The content of the report is based largely on two one day meetings of the Standards Task Force of the National Council on Education Standards and Testing held on September 19 and October 20. The report draws on a preliminary paper of the Task Force prepared for the September 23 meeting of the Council, a summary of the report prepared for discussion purposes for the October 21 meeting of the Council, and discussions of the Council, particularly at the September and October meetings. Insofar as possible this report represents a consensus of the Task Force but a consensus was not possible in all instances.

The views expressed in this appendix report reflect the work of this Task Force and are not necessarily those of the Council.

Legislative and Supporting Language

Sec. 4 Duties of the National Council on Education Standards and Testing Act (HR 2435) states: "The Council shall advise the American people on whether suitable specific education standards can be established such as world-class standards, for —

- the knowledge and skills that students should possess and that schools should impart in order that American students leave grades 4, 8, and 12 demonstrating competency in challenging subject matter including English, mathematics, science, history, and geography; and
- every school in America to ensure that all students learn to use their minds well so that they will be prepared for responsible citizenship, further learning, and productive employment in our modern economy; and..."

The House Report elaborates on Sec 2 of the Bill with very specific language:

[The Council shall] "... provide advice on (1)whether suitable specific education standards should and can be established, and..."

"It is the intent of the Committee that the Council address each of these issues in terms of its desirability and feasibility consistent with the bill's stated purpose (see section 2(a)of the bill)."

"...the Committee in no way endorses the proposition that national education standards... are either desirable or feasible. It is the purpose of the Council to examine a broad range of considerations with regard to these two issues and report their findings and recommendations to the Congress, the Secretary of Education and the National Goals Panel..."

Structure of the Report

This report responds directly to the issues concerning the desirability and feasibility of national education standards set out in HR 2435 and in the House Report. The report has three remaining parts:

- Part II proposes a definition of education standards which pays attention to the conceptualization of education standards set out in section 4 of the Bill.
- Part III considers the desirability of this Nation having "national education standards." This discussion responds to the questions set out in the House report on the Bill.
- Part IV considers whether it is feasible for this Nation to have national education standards. This discussion also responds to the House Bill report.

Three Underlying Assumptions

Before considering the definitions we want to underscore three important assumptions made in this report.

- *National vs. Federal Standards.* We assume from the language of the Bill and the Report and from early discussions of the Council that Congressional intent is that the education standards are to be national rather than federal. We support this interpretation. We take it to mean that, while the process for establishing and implementing the standards should be national in scope, it should not be under the control of the federal government, though the various parts of the federal government (the Congress and the administration) should be important participants. It also implies that the process for establishing the standards should reach out across the Nation to the many states and their communities.

- *Voluntary vs. Mandatory (Imposed) Standards.* If standards are national rather than federal, we assume that they are "voluntary" for the states. We support this interpretation. Only the federal government could have the authority to require states to use national education standards— and even that is unlikely in light of the language of the Constitution. Discretion for the adoption of the standards would continue to rest with the states, providing an important balance of power and responsibility. This is an extremely important point. It addresses the question in the House Committee Report which asks "what the benefits and liabilities are of imposing uniform national standards... on an education system where curriculum is traditionally controlled at the state and local level." The position taken here is that "education standards" would be voluntary, not mandatory or imposed nationally. The issue about the desirability of voluntary national standards, uniform or not, is naturally still important and will be fully considered. We remind the reader that being voluntary nationally would not stop individual states from making the standards mandatory for the school districts within their borders.

- *Challenging, not minimal education standards.* Undergirding the interest in national education standards is the idea that the content of the present curriculum in most United States schools lacks coherence, depth, and quality. Throughout this report we assume that national education standards will legitimately be "world class" in scope and quality. They must reflect high, not minimal, expectations for all of our Nation's students. If they are not challenging and of the highest quality, they are guaranteed to do more harm than good.

Definition of Education Standards

Education standards should respond to the fundamental questions: What should schools teach? What should students learn and how well should they learn it? And, in response to the text of the enabling legislation: What is the quality of a school's capacity to "ensure that all students learn to use their minds well...?" The term education standards is generic— it is important to develop a set of specific definitions for use by the Council and for responding to the important questions posed in the legislation and in the legislative report. The work of the National Council on Education Standards and Testing on education standards has focused primarily on five subject matter areas; English, mathematics, science, history, and geography. Within the context of a defined subject matter area we can distinguish several specific components designed to flesh out an overall definition of education standards.[2]

Overarching statement

The *overarching statement* should describe in brief and general terms a vision of the nature of the education standards for the content area. It should emphasize a theoretically and pedagogically coherent and engaging presentation of challenging, up-to-date subject matter and high expectations for achievement by all students, including an ultimate goal of world-class student achievement. The description of "Mathematical Power" in the new California Mathematics Framework is an example.

Content Standards

Content standards should set out the knowledge, skills, and other necessary understandings that schools should teach in order for all American students to attain high levels of competency in the subject matter. Generally, and for our purposes, what schools are expected to teach is equivalent to the knowledge, skills and other understandings that students are expected to learn in schools.[3] The National Council of Teachers of Mathematics (NCTM) *Curriculum and Evaluation Standards for School Mathematics*, the California Frameworks, the Syllabuses for the Advanced Placement Tests of the College Board, and the *Course of Study for Lower Secondary Schools* in Japan are all examples of *content standards*. For the purposes of the work of the Council, *content standards* should cover the entire range of pre-collegiate formal schooling (grades K-12) as do the NCTM *Curriculum and Evaluation Standards for School Mathematics* and the California Frameworks.

Student Performance Standards

Student performance standards should establish the degree or quality of student performance in the challenging subject matter set out in the *content standards*. In general, the development of such standards will require examples of a range of professionally judged student performances which serve as benchmarks for assessing the quality of a new student's performance. For example, the College Board Advanced Placement (AP) Tests are scored one (1) through five (5). Typically, a score of three (3)indicates that a student has performed well enough to pass a college level examination on the

---

2. The five subject matter areas are explicitly included in the legislation and in the report of the National Education Goals Panel.

3. Some authors and states use the term "curriculum framework" instead of the term "content standards." For our purposes we take the two terms to have identical meaning. Sometimes the term "achievement standards" is used to specify the content students are expected to learn while the term "content standards" is used to specify the content that schools are expected to teach. Here we are assuming that the two bodies of content are equivalent and thus we use the term "content standards" to refer to both what student are expected to learn and what schools are expected to teach.

subject, a score of four (4) indicates the student would have gotten a B in a college course examination, and a score of five (5) is superior performance equating to an A in college. The assignment of a level of performance on an AP Test requires an explicit comparison of the examination performance (essays, analyses of text, record of how difficult calculus problems are solved) with the prior performance of successful and unsuccessful college students on "equivalent" tests. The Task Force recommends that at least a three level scale of *student performance standards* will be necessary for grading assessments based on the education *content standards*. These might be labeled "competent performance," "excellent performance," and "world-class performance" standards. In order to establish the criteria for the final level, "world-class standards," we will need to gather information about the quality of the best student work in other nations.

School Delivery Standards

School delivery standards should set out criteria to enable local and state educators and policymakers, parents, and the public to assess the quality of a school's capacity and performance in educating their students in the challenging subject matter set out by the *content standards*. *School delivery standards* should provide a metric for determining whether a school "delivers" to students the "opportunity to learn" well the material in the *content standards*. Are the teachers in the school trained to teach the content of the standards? Does the school have appropriate and high quality instructional materials which reflect the *content standards*? Does the actual curriculum of the school cover the material of the *content standards* in sufficient depth for the students to master it to a high standard of performance? These input conditions are fundamental to providing all children the opportunity to learn the material of the *content standards*. Finally, on the outcome side, does the performance of the students in the school indicate that the school is successfully providing the "opportunity to learn" to all students? The concept of *school delivery standards* was developed by the Task Force to respond directly to the language of Sec. 4(1)(B) of HR 2435 which calls for "world-class standards for... every school in America to ensure that all students learn to use their minds well..." (see the *Legislative and Supporting Language* section of this report for more detail).

System Delivery Standards

System delivery standards should set out criteria for establishing the quality of a school system's (local, state, or national) capacity and performance in educating all students in the subject matter set out in the *content standards*. To some degree the *system delivery standards* for the Nation have already been developed by the National Education Goals Panel and the President in Goals 3 and 4, which establish targets for student achievement for the year 2000. The Task Force recommends that each state and local district establish their own achievement targets which, when summed, would enable the Nation to reach the National Goals.

Desirability of National Education Standards

The questions set out in the House Report focus on the issues of the desirability and feasibility of national education standards. In this section we focus on the series of questions which address the issue of the desirability of national standards.[4] For background and the consideration of the Council, however, we first briefly summarize some of the typical arguments for and against establishing national standards.

By and large these arguments are captured by three overarching questions:

Will national standards have a positive influence on student achievement and the quality of teachers and schools?

What is the potential impact of national standards on educational equity?

Are national standards appropriate given the American tradition of local control of curriculum and the existing wide variations in state and local resources for education?

These three overarching questions also provide a structure within which to address the Congressional questions set out in the House Report on HR 2435. After summarizing the "typical" pro and con arguments we turn to a more complete consideration of the three overarching questions.

Typical Arguments For and Against National Education Standards

Arguments Used to Support National Standards

- The international standing of the United States and the competitiveness of the United States economy, system of security, and diplomatic influence are national, not state or local. They require national attention to the development of the nation's human capital.

- National education standards will help assure that our increasingly diverse and mobile population will have the shared knowledge and values necessary to make our democracy work.

- National standards will help improve the quality of schools and of teacher professional development by providing a clear, common set of challenging goals and criteria for the allocation of scarce resources.

- National standards applicable for all children will help provide the impetus for realizing equality of educational opportunity across the Nation.

---

4. This section also addresses the questions set out in the September 20, 1991 letter to the Council from Congressmen Goodling and Kildee and from Senator Hatch which essentially repeats the questions in the House Committee Report, though in a different order.

- The establishment of challenging national standards will encourage states and localities to raise their educational expectations and standards.
- The states have scarce resources of talent and funds for the task of establishing their own standards and assessment systems. It would be far more efficient for the several states and localities to cooperate in a national approach than to create their own standards and assessment systems separately.

Common Arguments Against National Standards

- Our Nation's experience with centrally established standards (e.g., at the state level in education and at the state and national levels in other sectors) is that they are generally "minimum standards" which act to drag down the entire system. If such happened with national education standards, the entire system would suffer.
- If challenging national standards are established, but the strategies and resources for enabling students and schools to meet them are not put into place, the result will be a disservice to the Nation's students.
- The establishment of national standards would draw attention and resources away from the many, very positive state and local reforms that are now underway throughout the Nation.
- National standards will lead to a national curriculum, which will inhibit local and state creativity and initiative.
- The great diversity of the Nation, culturally and ethnically, and in regional traditions, make it impossible to have a single common set of education standards that would have widespread acceptance.

Will National Standards Have a Positive Influence on Student Achievement and the Quality of Teachers and Schools?

This addresses question 3 in the House Committee Report. [Is there] "any evidence that national education standards... promote improvements in educational achievement or in the ability of teachers to perform their jobs:" In order to answer this question it is important to consider both the current condition of schooling in American and a future condition where there are "voluntary national standards".

What is the Current Situation?

- *No explicit national education content or performance standards currently exist.* In the past, this Nation and its states have typically not established or required either challenging *content standards* or absolute standards of high student performance. Instead of setting challenging content expectations, instead of determining what level of performance represents a high level of mastery of content, we have relied on relative comparisons among schools, districts and states to give us an indication of how well we are doing. Our standardized tests generally tell us whether our students are above or below the average in the Nation or in the state, not whether their performance is superior either when compared to an international standard or to some *a priori* absolute standard.

- *We now have a de facto national curriculum of basic skills.* In the absence of common, well specified, demanding *content standards* and high expectations for students our Nation has gravitated toward a *de facto* national minimum competency curriculum. Except for the small percentage of our Nation's students who are headed for elite four year colleges, the Nation's *content standards* focus on basic reading and arithmetic skills, and relatively minimal amounts of factual information in science, geography and history.

- *This focus on basic skills reflects both intentional policy at state and local levels and the indirect influence of other forces* — including textbook publishers who cater to the lowest common denominator in content, test developers and educational administrators who use standardized tests which reinforce this focus, and teachers who have had neither adequate training nor appropriate role models in their own educational experience. In addition, some evidence indicates that teachers tend to focus their teaching on maximizing student performance on tests used for accountability purposes, which have typically emphasized basic competencies.

- *Public expectations for student performance are also sadly low.* As parents, as voters, and as members of the general public we settle for far less than do our counterparts in other developed Nations. Most state standards, where they exist, provide a floor, not a goal, for practice. High, or leading edge, requirements for education practice and student performance mean that for some period of time, and perhaps a lengthy period, most schools would be below standard, a situation typically viewed as politically intolerable. When high standards are proposed they are likely to also be followed by educator requests for more resources, making policymakers wary of initiating the cycle. This condition is beginning to change in a few states such as South Carolina and Vermont but the general fact is that, in a tight economy, the battle in states for higher education standards is very difficult to win. Typically, the voters are only lukewarm, and this makes the policymakers legitimately cautious.

- *The quality of our schools too often reflects our minimal expectations.* With the general exception of schools in affluent areas, many of our Nation's youth attend institutions that lack the human and material resources necessary to deliver to students a curriculum based on a challenging conception of content. In too many schools there is no science lab, students are not allowed to take home textbooks or other books to do their homework, and, of most concern, teachers are not trained well enough to understand, much less to teach, the kind of demanding material envisioned in the new *content standards*.

- *In summary, while they meet our expectations, at the present time our content, performance, and school delivery standards are mediocre at best.*

What Effect Does the Low Quality of Our Standards and Our Schools Have on Student Achievement?

It is difficult to imagine that our level of student achievement will improve greatly if we continue to support and implement our current minimal standards curriculum. Over the past 20 years student achievement has remained relatively flat or very slightly improved at best, with the exception that minority groups, particularly African Americans, have improved in basic skills areas. This indicates that the emphasis in the 1970s and early 1980s on *de facto* basic skills national standards — spurred and reinforced by direct state and local policy activity — had a distinct and positive effect on student achievement for those who could most benefit from it. Our overall level of student achievement, however, remains low-to-mediocre when compared with that of other developed nations, and by some indicators our relative position is even declining. If we are satisfied with this continuing level of mediocre achievement we can continue to ignore the challenge of setting higher and more challenging standards, for the content of instruction, for student performance, and for school quality. Unless we make a conscious effort to do so, however, we will continue to be the slaves of a *de facto* nationally accepted conception of scholastic achievement which is distinctly inferior to that of much of the rest of the developed world.

What Might Happen to Student Achievement and Teacher Behavior if There Were Challenging, Voluntary, National Education Standards?

• *Voluntary, challenging, national content and performance standards could stimulate improvements in state and local content and performance standards and expectations.* This, in turn, could have a positive effect on education practice in local schools and classrooms. The Council has heard testimony from the NCTM that the content and teaching standards that they have developed have had a great influence on the policies and practices of state and local boards of education as these groups have established the curricula of their jurisdictions. Similarly, though to a lesser extent, we understand that there is evidence that state and local communities have drawn from the work of the American Association for the Advancement of Science (AAAS) *Project 2061* for the development of national education standards for science.

• *But, content and performance standards alone cannot change student achievement and teacher performance.* Student achievement and teacher performance will not be greatly influenced by content and performance standards unless the standards are part of a coherent and systemic approach to improving instruction in the schools. Education policy efforts aimed at changing the *status quo* are generally short-term, unconnected to other policies and overall goals of the system, limited to a small set of schools or grades, and focused on particular problem areas rather than on the entire system. As a consequence they rarely have a sustaining effect. National standards, however, could lay the foundation for a different approach.

- Challenging national standards could set expectations for all schools and grades in key content areas, signalling the type of substantive changes we need system-wide in all of our schools and classrooms.

- A national examination system based on the *content standards* could reinforce and assess attainment of the standards. (See the companion report from the Assessment Task Force.)

- The *content* and *performance standards* could form the basis for other state policies, such as those dealing with adoption of instructional materials and teacher licensing and professional development. We would then have several interconnected policy efforts giving coherent guidance about teaching and learning around ambitious, not basic skills, outcomes. (See the companion report from the Implementation Task Force.)

- *Most important, student achievement and teacher performance will only change in a dramatic way if existing and future teachers are trained to be able to teach the challenging content in the new national standards.* Though it would be important that new instructional materials based on the new standards be developed and that schools have the other material resources necessary to teach the *content standards*, none of this will help unless there is a dramatic effort to prepare teachers to teach the new content. Most public school teachers do not have the deep, sophisticated understanding of subject matter required to teach the content indicated by the kind of education standards proposed here. The new content expectations would also call for new ways of teaching, for strategies that actively engage students. Most teachers are not used to teaching in such ways. They have few opportunities and little time to learn on the job. Nor does pre-service professional development meet these challenges. If national standards are to spur improved teaching and learning, they will need reinforcement by extensive and carefully developed professional development activities.

- *Evidence about the effect of ambitious, coherent instructional reforms on teaching and student achievement is positive but not plentiful.* Some states, notably California, New York, Vermont, Kentucky, Arizona and Arkansas, are aligning challenging content objectives and assessment. However, almost all of these efforts are very recent; most do not yet tie teacher professional development and instructional materials policies to the curriculum/assessment strategies. This is a very different situation than exists in many other developed nations where there are coherent policy systems linking content standards to instructional materials, examination systems and professional development. That there are currently few coherent systems designed to upgrade instruction in the American states is a major reason for the Council's existence.

    The little direct evidence that does exist suggests that ambitious content standards reinforced by assessment and other policies have the potential to improve schooling. Preliminary data indicate that the California mathematics framework actively influences local policy and instruction. A study using the International Education

Assessment's Second International Mathematics Study (SIMS) found that teachers in nations with more coherent curricular guidance were more consistent, more alike in the topics they covered, indicating an influence of the common focus. Analyses of national survey data indicate that secondary schools in this Nation which have coherent approaches, such as common curricula and shared goals, tend to be somewhat more successful than other schools in limiting absenteeism and dropping out, improving achievement performance, and reducing performance differences among students.

- *In summary, will the adoption of new, explicitly challenging education standards affect student achievement?* Perhaps not directly, but the odds of our Nation's expectations and commitment changing without committing ourselves to challenging standards are practically zero. Moreover, as our experience in the 1970s and early 1980s with minimum competencies indicates, a common set of expectations and standards can affect teacher behavior and student achievement outcomes. This suggests the possibility that more challenging content, performance, and delivery standards which were implicitly or explicitly adopted by the Nation, in concert with serious systemic reform efforts, would have a positive effect for all students.

Educational Equity for Students

This section addressees question 7 in the House Report: "Whether support that would provide educationally disadvantaged children, handicapped children, and children with limited English proficiency the opportunity to succeed should be a part of any effort to implement national education standards...?

It is trite but important to say that a major part of the justification for national education standards must rest on their promise for improving the quality of the educational experiences of the most needy in our society.

Where Does the Nation Stand?

During the 1970s and throughout the 1980s, the achievement gap between majority and minority and rich and poor has been closing. Gains made in the past twenty-five years by African American, Hispanic American, and low income children in partially closing the achievement gap with middle income whites have been due both to changes in social and economic conditions and to a national focus on basic skills which sought to equalize the quality of education offered to students of different backgrounds. The scores of minorities and low income students have risen while the scores of the middle income and majority students have stayed essentially level.

Over the past decade the social, political and economic circumstances of many low income and minority families have worsened. Moreover, the basic skills emphasis in schools is being legitimately criticized for its failure to develop in all students the higher levels of learning and more complex skills necessary in a technologically advanced society. As a consequence, many local districts and schools have instituted reforms that attempt to emphasize higher order thinking and a more challenging curriculum.

Locally Initiated Reforms Might Widen the Gap

As educationally progressive as the local reforms to improve the quality of the curriculum may be, they could also place many minorities and the poor at a new disadvantage because the poor and minorities in the society are typically the last to benefit from locally generated reforms — if they benefit at all. Districts and schools with large numbers of poor and minority students often have less discretionary money to stimulate reform, less well trained teachers, and more day-to-day problems that drain administrative energy away from constructive reforms. In conjunction with the increasing numbers of children in poverty and the depressingly bad economic condition of many cities the new reforms could well lead to substantial new increases in the achievement gap.[5]

This outcome will almost certainly occur if the changes in the schools are initiated one school and one district at a time. If, however, the changes were expected to apply roughly equally across the schools within a very large district or across the schools and districts within a state, there is some hope that greater equality of opportunity would result.

Common, Challenging Standards and High Expectations Could Serve Equity Well

The opportunity for a condition of equal expectations could be enhanced under a system (large district, state or Nation) which had a common set of challenging *content standards* and high *performance standards* for all of its students. Within such a system the nature of inequalities in resources necessary for preparing students to reach the common standards would be more easily exposed than under the present system where the expectations differ across schools and districts. Differences in the capacity (knowledge, experience) of teachers to teach the common material and in the quality of textbooks and school resources to support teaching the common material would be more likely to be evident.

School Delivery Standards Are Critical

Nonetheless, if not accompanied by measures to ensure equal opportunity to learn, national *content* and *performance standards* could help widen the achievement gap between the advantaged and the disadvantaged in our society. If national *content* and *performance standards* and assessment are not accompanied by clear school delivery standards and policy measures designed to afford all students an equal opportunity to learn, the concerns about diminished equity could easily be realized. Standards and assessments must be accompanied by policies that provide access for all students to high quality resources, including appropriate instructional materials and well-prepared teachers. High *content* and *performance standards* can be used to challenge all students with the same

---

5. The Nation may already be seeing the consequences of increased poverty among its children. The most recent National Assessment of Education Progress shows a substantial increase in the gap between majority and African American children in reading and mathematics achievement for the first time in almost two decades. Almost all of the increase in the gap comes from a decline in the scores of African American students.

expectations, but high expectations will only result in common high performance if all schools provide high quality instruction designed to meet the expectations.[6]

Federal Programs Can Help

Federal programs for the needy could offer critical assistance for helping needy students meet high *performance standards*. For twenty-five years, equal opportunity in this Nation has meant something other than evenhanded treatment. Equal opportunity means extra attention, resources and assistance for those with special problems and needs. Through Chapter 1 (originally Title 1) of the Elementary and Secondary Education Act (ESEA); Public Law 94-142; and Title VII of the ESEA, the federal government has shown its commitment to provide special support for economically disadvantaged, handicapped, and limited English speaking students. Many states have parallel programs.

Nothing about national standards suggests eliminating or reducing these programs. In fact, given the renewed importance of opportunity to learn in the context of consensus about what we want students to learn, these programs should take on additional importance. Students with special problems will continue to need extra help if they are to have equal opportunity. It will be very important, however, to consider the form of the assistance offered through the federal categorical programs. In the past these programs have often been designed to operate independently of the central curriculum and instructional program of the schools. In the future, under a system of challenging *content* and *performance standards*, the federal categorical programs must be designed and implemented in a way that reinforces the opportunities for the most needy students to perform to the highest possible level on the common *content standards*.

Diversity in States and Local Districts

This section addresses questions 2 and 5 in the House report. "What the benefits and liabilities are of imposing uniform national standards ... on an educational system where curriculum is traditionally controlled at the state and local level?" and "Whether uniform national standards are appropriate when there are wide variations in the resources available to school system across states?"

We have already addressed the issue of "imposing" national standards in our earlier discussion of "voluntary vs. mandatory" education standards. Here we assume the standards would be voluntary but consider the desirability of developing and recommending them at the national level rather than leaving this task solely to the states and localities. We consider first the desirability of a national consensus around specified content goals and then we move to the issue of variation in state and local resources.

---

6. There are a large number of examples of situations where poor and minority students have been given challenging, high quality content and instruction and performed to high levels of achievement. The story of Jaime Escalante's work in high school mathematics may be the best known.

What Would Be the Effect of a National Consensus Around Education Standards on Our Educational System?

- *The Task Force believes that a national consensus around education standards could enhance the sense of national identity and community we need as our Nation becomes increasingly diverse.* National standards could form a core, to which states, localities and schools could add standards tailored to the needs and interests of their students and communities. Given such a consensus and system, we as a Nation could accommodate diversity and still have a means of achieving a prime purpose of public schooling: creating an informed citizenry that shares underlying values about democracy.

- *Of course, there is a danger and counter-argument, namely that national standards might be too centralizing, might in fact constrain states, communities and schools from responding effectively to the diverse goals and needs of their constituents and students.* Several safeguards in the system could prevent such a situation from materializing.

First, as stated previously, the standards would have to be national and voluntary, not federal or mandatory.

Second, the standards should be developed and viewed as a common core that, where adopted, would be enhanced through considerable state and local flexibility. For example, while national standards should be sufficiently detailed so as not to be vague, they should be sufficiently general so as to permit schools and teachers to develop their own detailed curricula. One form that this flexibility might take would be to build in state and local choices and options, as in the sequencing of subjects or in the choice of literature within each genre. Another form would be the addition by states and localities of their own unique content and performance expectations to reflect their own histories and populations. This notion of flexibility within a common core is supported by a variety of evidence. Research in the United States, for example, shows that central curricula are only one of many influences on teaching and that ambitious new state content frameworks are being interpreted by teachers in a variety of ways. At the same time, experiences from other countries also provide various practical models for building local flexibility into a national framework.

A third factor mitigating against over-centralization is that the national standards could build on the already significant work done by a number of states in reaching consensus about ambitious student outcomes. California, New York, Kentucky, Vermont, South Carolina and other states have developed or are beginning to develop standards that national groups could adapt, adopt, mirror, or borrow from. By building on more locally derived consensus, the national standards would not prescribe as much as they would reinforce what has already been agreed to.

Are National Standards Appropriate Given Wide Variations in State and Local Fiscal and Human Resources?

Advocates argue that a benefit of a set of voluntary, challenging, national standards is that where adopted they will provide an underlying commonality and standard of quality for the education of our Nation's youth, thus serving to protect the national public interest. Such, at least, is the overriding goal. A mitigating factor in achievement of this goal is the fact that diversity in student populations and variation in state and local resources will contribute to observed variation in performance and delivery standards among and within states.

- *Will challenging national standards serve as common goals for states and localities which have widely varying resources?* Variation in resources should not be used to justify and excuse wide variation in the quality of content presented or the levels of student performance, as now occurs. The Task Force believes that, instead, well defined and challenging national standards (content, performance, and delivery) can serve both to point out problems and to establish clear targets for all states and localities to strive for. This is a similar argument to that used earlier in the discussion of equity issues. A primary condition that must be met, of course, is that states adopt the standards. Our sense is that this will depend on the quality of the standards. If the standards are of the highest quality, there will be great moral and political pressure on most states to adopt them. One by-product of adopting and implementing the common standards will be that comparisons among states in student performance, which already exist and will continue to exist, would have greater validity and legitimacy. This fact could cut both ways as states consider whether or not to adopt the common standards.

- *States would not be confined to their own resource base in striving toward common, higher standards.* States and localities could work together — through regional consortia or other cooperative groupings as many already are — to overcome differences and deficiencies in resources. Such cooperation could easily lead to higher quality curricula, instructional materials, teacher professional development, and/or assessment instruments in order to help ensure higher levels of student performance on the *content* and *performance standards* in all the participating localities.

Feasibility and the Standard-Setting Process

This part of the report addresses the questions on feasibility in the House report.

Feasibility

Can this Nation develop high quality content, performance, and delivery standards?

Testimony and Direct Evidence Indicate That It Is Possible to Develop High-Quality and Challenging National Education Standards.

The National Council on Education Standards and Testing has heard considerable testimony from teachers and other education professionals in the five subject matter areas, from states, and from the developers and the governing board of the National Assessment of Educational Progress (NAEP). In addition, the Council has received information from the College Board about their AP and Achievement examinations and from a variety of sources about the experiences of other nations. This testimony and evidence indicates that:

- *High quality and demanding national content standards have been and can be developed.* The NCTM standards are an existence proof for the United States for national *content standards* which encompass Kindergarten through Twelfth grade. The California Frameworks are examples of high quality *content standards* for our most populous and diverse state.
- *Demanding performance standards for students have been and can be developed.* The *performance standards* for the AP examinations are an example in the United States. (For more discussion of this issue see the report on assessment.)
- *The Task Force believes that appropriate delivery standards could be developed for meeting the demands of challenging content and performance standards, but there is little relevant experience in the United States.* In the United States, delivery standards (i.e. accreditation standards) have typically been developed independently of the curriculum since there are no common content standards. For the United States, the specification and use of delivery standards associated with common *content standards* (e.g., high quality curricular materials and professional development programs based on the content standards) would be breaking new ground except in rare areas. One exception is the guidelines for instruction proposed by the NCTM which is associated with the NCTM *Standards*. Other exceptions are the materials associated with Advanced Placement courses and the International Baccalaureate.

Although Examples of Challenging Frameworks and Demanding Performance Standards Exist in the United States, this still Does Not Demonstrate the Feasibility of Developing Challenging Educational Standards Which Are to be Explicitly Adopted as National (Although Voluntary)

Is not the Nation too ethnically and culturally diverse and are not our traditions too rooted in state and local governance and control to allow us to reach the national "consensus" over *content* and *performance standards* that would make their development ultimately worthwhile? There are a number of key issues here:

- *A byproduct of this argument raises the possibility that national standards, developed by consensus, will not be challenging.* Experience in education and in other sectors teaches us that standards set by governments are likely to be set at minimum levels, the lowest common denominator. Current debates over the extent to which content must reflect the racial and ethnic diversity of the

Nation, and over the extent to which each school's focus must reflect its own racial and ethnic makeup, underscore the difficulty of reaching "consensus" except at a superficial level. In addition, "consensus," and therefore acceptance and ownership, is endangered by disagreement over controversial curriculum issues, like the teaching of evolution. However, a variety of experiences provide counter-examples to these arguments.

- *The fact that challenging and high quality content standards, even in sensitive and particularly complex areas such as science and history/social studies, have been developed in a state like California, which has great diversity, indicates that the challenge of diverse opinions can be overcome by hard work and careful attention and respect for differences of opinion among the various interests.* California has been able to adopt sophisticated and complex curriculum frameworks in mathematics, social studies, and science. We are not suggesting that the task will be easy — witness New York state's recent experience with their History framework — but we do believe that it is feasible.

- *The fact that the NCTM as a professional group has reached national "consensus" on content standards is a positive though not entirely convincing argument for our ability to bridge the strong state and local traditions of our Nation.* The nationwide agreement among professionals in mathematics and mathematics teaching reached by the NCTM on very challenging content expectations are echoed by the experiences of the several subject area standards Task Forces formed by the National Board for Professional Teaching Standards (NBPTS). Neither of these efforts reflects any watering down of content or avoidance of controversial issues. As the NCTM standards or closely cloned versions of the standards are adopted by more and more state Boards of Education, the argument for the power of compelling, high quality, yet voluntary, national standards becomes more convincing.

- *It is clear from these examples (and from others such as NAEP) that it is feasible to develop national education standards which are far more challenging than the de facto, minimal, basic skills standards which presently drive much of American education.*

Standard-Setting Process

Even with these examples of the feasibility of developing challenging, voluntary, national standards, however, we do not know the extent to which the standards will be embraced by the public and thus the extent to which they will ultimately affect our Nation's schools. To an important degree, the Task Force believes that the extent of the influence will depend upon the level of ownership of the new standards felt by the Nation's education profession, federal, local and state policy makers, parents of all children, and the public. Ownership of the new national education standards by these various constituents will be an essential cornerstone of the Nation's commitment to change the content and quality of instruction in our schools. Moreover, ownership of the new national standards will generate a vision to guide the actions of state and local policy makers, to focus reform and the use of resources in schools, and to provide purpose and content to teacher professional development.

How Can a Process for Developing National Education Standards Be Created that Will Ensure that All Interested Participants, Including Teachers, Have an Opportunity to be Heard?

For national standards to form the basis of a shared national vision of what schools can deliver they must accurately reflect what we as a Nation want students to achieve. They must represent a true shared understanding of our goals for student academic achievement. Yet, how can we expect policy makers, the public, and many education professionals to aspire to new and challenging standards if they have not had the opportunity to be exposed to them? In order for the public to embrace challenging standards of "world-class" quality, it must be given the opportunity to engage in a national discussion with concrete examples of high quality content and student performance. Expert judgement must be discussed, debated, and refined by widespread public participation. Parents, business leaders, citizens, political leaders, university educators, and even students throughout the Nation should be involved.

Approaches to Standard-Setting

While there are a variety of ways that a standard-setting process could be conducted, there are three main approaches.

- *The first approach is the most efficient in cost and time: it begins at the national level and relies largely on professional input from throughout the Nation.* This is the model that has traditionally be used by NAEP though recently the NAEP process has broadened significantly. In this model no direct attempt is made to influence the minds and hearts of most state and local educators and policy makers, parents, or the public at large.
- *The second model begins at the local and state level and generates existing documents and concerns that are synthesized at the national level.* This model has the advantage of building on existing work and has some substantial grassroots input.
- *The third model starts with professional judgement and examples from the national level and then looks to the state and local level for guidance from a wide variety of sources.* In this third model prototypic education standards would move through at least one and preferably two iterations from the national to the state and local levels and back for continued refinement. As the iterative process continues the hope is that ownership by all groups across the Nation would substantially increase. This is similar to the model recommended by the technical advisory group to Goal 3 of the National Education Goals Panel.

Task Force Recommendation

The Task Force recommends the third model. Though we recognize that it would be the most costly in time and money we believe the investment would be worthwhile. Our strong sense is that this model offers the best chance for engaging a wide spectrum of the public and, consequently, has the greatest promise for helping in the successful implementation of the new, challenging education standards throughout the Nation.

Report of the Assessment Task Force

Introduction

Part of the Council's congressional mandate is to report on the following issues:

"... whether, while respecting state and local control of education, an appropriate system of voluntary national tests or examinations should and can be established, such as American achievement tests, that will provide prompt, accurate information to parents, educators, and policymakers on the progress being made toward the specific education standards by individual students, schools, school systems, states, and the Nation as a whole (if such standards can be established). The goal of any such system shall be to foster good teaching and learning, as well as to monitor performance."

"A discussion of the validity, reliability, fairness, and costs of implementing a system of voluntary national tests or examinations shall also be included in such report."

It is our purpose to consider the desirability and feasibility of a system to assess the National Education Standards. Our report will address

---

The views expressed in this appendix report reflect the work of this Task Force and are not necessarily those of the Council.

the validity, reliability, fairness, cost, and, particularly, potential impact on students with special needs. The report is organized into five sections: 1)background, where we provide context for our deliberations and discuss important terms including assessment purposes, uses and misuses; 2)desirability, where we consider the present assessment system, a sample of arguments for and against a system to assess national standards, a set of desired principles and requirements for the system, and propose state and national functions and roles in a new system; 3)feasibility, where we identify issues that must be solved to assure feasibility; 4)implementation, where we propose early steps to be taken; and 5)issues, where we discuss concerns the members of the Task Force wish to bring to the attention of the Council.

Background

Context

For many Americans, the vision of a renewed educational system includes assessment as a central component. They desire a system where assessment challenges all students and educators to do their best, opens up new opportunities and accomplishments for everyone, and provides incentives to improve the quality of America's schools. These hopes arise from a variety of perspectives — from the big picture — that our Nation cannot permit its education system to erode if we are to flourish in the future; and from close-up experience — that education is fundamentally a student-by-student proposition where rich accomplishments, verified by assessments, can develop a child's abilities and sense of worth in positive and powerful ways.

We approach these compelling goals for assessment with many reasonable reservations. First, we recognize that any national system must honor the traditions of local and state responsibility for education and, consequently, for flexibility and adaptation. Second, because of our extensive experience with tests, data of other types, and accountability attempts, we realize we must have high standards for the quality and fairness of the assessments. Third, an assessment system of the scope imagined is a new enterprise for our Nation, so we must make sure we avoid the salient harms unintentionally created by assessment systems in the past.

Our deliberations have been sometimes contentious — aspirations differ; reservations vary; evidence is credible to some and but not to others. We have omitted the technical details of our disagreements and have described basic principles about which we agree — principles that must be followed if any assessment system is to provide benefits while offering needed protection. If requirements we propose are met, we believe we may succeed. We believe we have a place for this Nation to begin.

Purposes, Uses, and Misuses of Assessment

A system to assess the national standards may have many purposes, among which we distinguish five:

Raising Standards for American Education

- monitoring progress toward National Education Goals
- holding schools or students accountable for performance
- certifying individual achievement and accomplishments
- improving instruction
- evaluating the effectiveness of schooling or reforms

Each of these five functions is assumed to be in the service of larger goals — the improvement of our children's accomplishments and the quality of their educational experience. Nonetheless, these five functions are distinct and impose different requirements on an assessment system.

The following section is offered to explain frequently used terms as well as to help the Council use the common language when discussing the content of the report.

Monitoring

Sound educational policy decisions require dependable information about achievement of the National Education Goals. Ideally this information provides an independent and relevant picture of educational progress. This information can be acquired in cost-effective ways that do not require the assessment of every student or school every year. Examples of monitoring assessment systems are the National Assessment of Educational Progress (NAEP) and many existing state assessment programs.

Accountability

Tests and assessments are frequently viewed as means of holding schools and educators accountable for student achievement. Test-based accountability has, in the past, focused attention on the goals and content that are tested. Unless tests focus on the full range of important outcomes, curriculum and instruction become narrowed. Accountability does not have to depend only upon test results. For example, we could hold schools and educators accountable for promoting high levels of competence in certain subject matters and for assuring that all children have a wide range of important learning opportunities in untested areas, such as foreign language and the arts. Systems could be held accountable to assure that qualified teachers are teaching in given subject areas. What makes accountability problematic in every domain is the pressure it creates to find inappropriate short-cuts in order to produce "good results." The higher the stakes, the greater the pressure. Thus it is important that the assessments, as fully as possible, reflect all important goals. Furthermore, we must be vigilant that the integrity of the assessment is protected against corruption of various sorts. For these reasons, the same assessments can almost never provide simultaneously good monitoring and accountability information.

Certification

The use of assessments to certify the accomplishments of individual students is undertaken for many purposes: to develop highly accomplished members of our society, to demonstrate and focus the impact of educational services, and to encourage student effort to achieve valued ends. For all of these purposes, it is essential that standards of achievement, the steps that will help students progress toward the required standards, and the benefits of certification be communicated openly to students, teachers, parents, and the public. Because of the consequences of certification for an individual's future, the certification purpose of assessment also carries with it the strictest technical criteria for validity and fairness. Standards and the tests that measure them for one individual's certification need to be equivalent to the standards and tests used for any other individual. Furthermore, certification assessments that tie consequences to individual performance — for instance, denial of high school diplomas — or are required for particular employment, have specific legal precedents that set useful and important standards for instructional environments or the relationship of the assessment to actual on-the-job skills.

Instructional Improvement

Assessment can be an integral part of effective teaching. Indeed, the best assessments and instruction expect the same active involvement of students in problem solving and the development of skills and understanding. Assessments that are used to improve instruction, however, are likely to differ from those used for the other purposes noted above in a number of important ways. The key audiences for assessments intended to improve day-to-day instruction within individual classrooms are students, teachers, and parents. Intensive teacher involvement in the development, scoring, and use of assessment information may be critical to this instructional improvement function. Assessments used for this purpose must provide timely feedback on student performance to both teachers and students, and they must provide both teachers and students with clear models of the learning and performances that are desired. In addition, the needed frequency of assessment is likely to constrain the usefulness of external tests more for this purpose than for the others, because teachers must make myriad and frequent decisions about instructional content and style.

Evaluation of Schooling or Programs

The evaluation of schooling requires more than only dependable information about student academic achievement; it may also require assessment of non-cognitive outcomes, like attitudes, levels of participation, and interests as well as clear information on parental education, poverty and other non-school factors. Assessments designed for monitoring purposes can often be used in evaluation studies, but, in addition, it is almost always expected that the evaluation will allow inferences about the likely causes of assessed performance. These causes or influences may be the impact of particular reform interventions, in combination with student background factors. To draw strong conclusions, it may be necessary to collect longitudinal information on the same students to assess their growth in achievement and other desired outcomes. Uses of such evaluation may be formative, to improve the particular program or

schooling effort, or summative, to make a go-no-go decision about a
particular program or strategy.

High-Stakes Use

Much conversation in assessment focuses on high-stakes uses of
assessments. But what constitutes high stakes? The phrase means
different things to different people. In the present context, however,
the key is whether performance on the assessment has substantial
consequences for participants in the educational system. The
consequences of an assessment might be desired by or imposed on
students, teachers, or administrators. A clear form of high-stakes use
is individual certification, in which some important event — for
instance, graduation from high school, admission to college, or
selection for employment — is made contingent on performance on an
examination. Other relatively high-stakes uses include proposals to
make teachers' compensation or state financial aid to schools or
districts contingent on scores. High stakes occur when test results are
used to compare schools in choice programs. An essential and
complicating lesson of the test-based reforms of the 1980s, however,
is that tests can become high stakes even in the absence of severe,
externally announced sanctions of this sort. In some instances,
publicity alone was sufficient to spark a chain of events sufficient to
make tests high stakes, for example, by inducing district or building
administrators to use test scores as an important criterion for staff
evaluation. Whenever consequences of test scores are substantial for
individuals, issues of validity, reliability, and fairness become more
difficult. Where high stakes are more a matter of perception than
actual consequences, issues such as fairness may be less salient, but
the risk of unintended deleterious effects on instruction and less
trustworthy results are substantial nonetheless.

Test Misuse

Concerns for misuse of tests and other assessments are at the core of
many reservations about the implementation of mandated
assessments as instruments of national policy. Why is this issue so
important? References such as the *Standards for Educational and
Psychological Tests* and the report of the National Academy of
Education emphasize, among other issues, that the validity of an
instrument or assessment does not solely reside in the test itself, but
depends as well upon the ways test results are used. At the most
global level, misuse occurs when results are used for unintended
purposes. And it is important to note that significant writers in the
field believe that differences between appropriate use and misuse are
not always crystal clear. One kind of misuse involves an inappropriate
interpretation of the purpose of the test. For example, a misuse
occurs when tests that are intended to provide information on
strengths and weaknesses to improve instruction are used to label
students. Another misuse might result from using a measure with a
weak base of evidence, for instance, in making certain certification
decisions based on a single, weakly validated measure. A third misuse
involves the consequences of using given measures to make decisions
about students resulting in unfair decisions. Misuse is a paramount

concern because if misused, tests can undermine efforts to improve education and can harm children. Misuse is important because it may lead to erroneous judgments about educational performance. Tests are not valid in and of themselves; rather, they are valid only to the extent that they provide a firm basis for reaching specific conclusions. A test that is well suited to supporting one type of conclusion may be entirely inadequate for supporting another. One use — or misuse — of a test may undermine its validity for another use. For example, using a test for accountability — and thereby encouraging teaching to the test — will generally undermine the validity of that test for monitoring progress. While there are many other instances that can be cited of test misuse, it is important that reasonable steps are taken in any proposed system to avoid the harms caused by test misuse.

Desirability of System to Assess the National Standards

Present State of the United States Assessment System

Education in the United States is test-happy. We expend significant resources on student testing, data collection of "hard" information, program evaluations, and report preparation — all undertaken nominally to meet the major purposes of assessment. Few believe that the present system is successful. Information is inconsistent and often incoherent. The information provided is seldom timely and there is little articulation among tests given for elementary, middle, and secondary school students. Despite the preoccupation with testing, we have no real assessment system. How can we explain our predicament?

- Many external tests and assessments float free of the core reality of classrooms, curriculum, and teaching practices. Teachers are expected to "use" test results to improve their day-to-day instruction, but rarely are assessments, curricula, texts, and teaching practices aligned. Tests and textbooks often emphasize different goals and content. Moreover, teachers are taught in teacher education programs "book-learning" about tests, but not much about how such information can be of practical use. Sadly, knowledge provided by test results has not been "power" for teachers.

- Test-based accountability, while a compelling idea, has seldom worked in its present form. Standards of performance may be lowered so that schools will not look too bad. Test content is simplified. The press and public make incorrect inferences from test scores. Because the tests may not be aligned with curriculum and instructional practices, there are no clear guidelines for how teachers can use the test information to improve instruction. Consequently, teachers, quite rationally, may teach children "test-taking skills" rather than subject matter. Valuable instructional time is spent practicing similar items or tasks as on the test — a reasonable but ultimately counterproductive alternative because tests always are limited in coverage. Effects are worse when test items are shallow or trivial. The curriculum that children are taught constricts to what is on these tests.

- Some but not all analysts believe, therefore, that our tests can be blamed for much of the poor teaching and low quality materials found in some of our schools. Many tests provide a model of "quick, right answer," piece-meal learning, and artificial divisions of subject matter into microskills. These tests are thought to exemplify a discredited view of learning — a view that basic skills must be learned before complex thinking. While it is arguable that tests alone are responsible for the type of instruction found in all too many schools, it is clear that we have not sufficiently explored ways to assess students' deeper knowledge of subject matter, complex problem solving, and clear communication. And what about good citizenship, commitment to hard work, and team building? What about subjects other than the core subjects?

- Even high quality tests may be misused. They provide an illusion of precision. Federal testing requirements for program services and accountability result in classifying students in ways that frequently retard student progress rather than support it. Assessments have included material that is biased against children of different races and gender. Mandated tests have a particularly bad track record with Limited English Proficient (LEP) students, disadvantaged students, and other special populations. Some test misuse in schools occurs without sanction, despite the dismay of test experts and commercial testing companies.

- The costs of our present system are high, not so much because the tests and information are expensive but because they are so rarely used to make things better. Bureaucracies demand accountability reports for Federal and state funds. These reports seldom inform policy but provide the appearance of "bottom-line" management.

- A bright spot is the NAEP, which in its present model with current constraints provides reasonable information on the quality of the Nation's achievement. It functions well as an independent mechanism to monitor national and state progress toward the National Education Goals, particularly Goal 3. NAEP can do this because it is not burdened with more than one purpose. If we were to add accountability to its purpose of monitoring national progress, its continued utility for monitoring would be questionable.

- The present system also has many resources in the form of expertise of commercial developers, and innovative new assessments coming from them and from the schools, universities, and dedicated individuals committed to improving the way we assess students and use results.

In sum, our present system of assessment has substantial weaknesses as well as some strengths, and many of us believe that it cannot serve as a major impetus for fundamental change. The issue before the Council is whether, and to what degree and under what conditions, a new assessment system would be better able to assist in the current reform agenda.

We have at least two reasonable alternatives: 1)not to use assessment as an instrument of educational policy or 2)to redesign a new strategy from the ground up to assess national education standards.

Arguments for a New Assessment System

A sense of urgency coupled with persistent American optimism has resulted in a raft of arguments for a new assessment system. Some arguments are put forth with a particular vision and belief that it is most critical to change the form of the tests from multiple choice tests to performance-based tasks. Others hold that attaching real consequences to performance is essential. Below is a summary of the range of aspirations for a new assessment system (but not necessarily a single national test). Notice that there are conflicts and tensions among some of these arguments. The first set of arguments focus on assessments in general.

- Assessments are the critical instrument of educational policy. They are a cost-effective lever for changing the system. They give us something to shoot for. They let us know how we are doing. They will motivate students, their parents, and the system to work harder.
- To motivate students and teachers to work harder, new assessments must have consequences for the world outside of school as well as that inside of school. If assessments count, in the job market or for college application, students will try harder.
- Both special education and LEP students have been excluded from assessments. The major problem with this approach has been that these students are then placed "outside of accountability." A more inclusive approach towards assessment is needed if equity concerns are to be respected.
- America needs a wake-up call. In fact, each local community needs a wake-up call. Only clear test results will convince local communities and parents that their own school and their own children may have serious problems.
- Common assessments are an essential component to open up choice of public schools or education program to parents.
- An assessment system will give renewed meaning to high school diplomas and restore public confidence in educational institutions.
- Recent polls show that the public wants some form of national testing. They want to be able to know how kids in different schools, districts, and states compare against common standards.
- Tests can help to overcome inequity. Students should be judged on how they perform and not on other characteristics. Unless all students are helped to achieve high standards, we will perpetuate, if not exacerbate, the class and racial divisions in this Nation.
- If the education goals and standards are going to be more than rhetoric, we must assess our progress toward their achievement.
- Education has not improved because tests have few real consequences for students. Students must be held to high standards

and not passed through the system because of time spent in classrooms.

- Test-based accountability is the "bottom line" of education. Until teachers and administrators are made to feel responsible for their students' performance, they have few incentives to change what they do.

- Our evaluation systems have too many mind-numbing procedural requirements. We need to allow more creativity in the system by holding schools responsible for outcomes and let schools develop ways to achieve them.

Some arguments for a national system of assessment depend upon a specific vision of assessment and tests as part of a larger educational reform effort. Critical to this view is the importance of aligning testing to curriculum and instruction. Arguments in support of this view include the following:

- Our international partners in Europe and Asia have education systems that produce a high level of literacy and competence. Testing linked to curriculum is a component of these systems. A national examination system, based on clear curricula and on examinations that can be prepared for, could also be used in this country.

- Aligning standards, curricula, and tests will permit clear communication to all constituencies in the educational community. Information from measures will make sense and educational resources can be coherently focused to rapidly improve our status. Evidence in support of this view can be seen, for one segment of the student population, in the recent report of Advanced Placement Tests.

Other arguments hinge on the use of a particular form of assessment as a way to integrate curriculum, teaching, learning, and assessment: performance assessment. Performance assessment requires students to complete challenging tasks that call for deep understanding of subject matter, problem solving, and communication. These tasks may be conceived as extended projects, hands-on demonstrations such as conducting experiments, or portfolios, where students include evidence of a range of accomplishments or their developed expertise. Currently numerous local and state education agencies are developing such assessments. Among the advantages cited are:

- Assessments can be more engaging for students and more understandable to parents and the community.

- Working on the development and the evaluation of performance tasks provides an invaluable experience for teachers. Performance assessment brings together assessment and teaching in a powerful, concrete way.

- Scoring performance assessments enables teachers to develop a clear understanding of the qualities of successful work, i.e., what it means and how to recognize it. Students can use the scoring system to assess their own work and internalize high standards.

- Performance tasks provide models for teachers of the best instructional practice. Even if a teacher does not help design a performance-based assessment, she or he will be given a dramatic new way to conceive of and to improve instruction.

- Performance assessments that are cumulative encourage students to take responsibility for their own learning by reflecting on their own work.

- Because of the integral relationship of performance assessment and learning, the harms previously associated with mandated assessments will be mitigated.

- Numerous local and state education agencies are developing these assessments already, with reports of great enthusiasm by participating teachers. We have an eager clientele for educational assessment of this form.

There is considerable sentiment, momentum, and passion for the development of new assessment systems.

Arguments Against a New Assessment System

Yet there is no shortage of arguments against a national system of assessment. Parallel to the arguments by assessment proponents, opponents frame their objections in the light of certain assumptions about the planned system. Again, let's begin with the most general concerns — pertinent to almost any system of assessment that may be envisioned.

- Externally mandated tests have not worked in this country. There is no reason to believe they will work this time.

- A major danger of a national system is that it will be asked to fulfill too many purposes simultaneously — monitoring progress toward national goals, instructional improvement, accountability, and certification. No single measure can meet these multiple responsibilities.

- We already know our system is in trouble. Let's fix it before we test it. We do not have resources enough to spend on teaching, books, and chalk.

- The environments from which some children come — with conditions of poverty, poor health, and inadequate family support — make our educational system less likely to be successful with tests or without them.

- A national assessment system will exacerbate rather than solve the equity problem. Sports metaphors notwithstanding, having tests will not level the playing field. Disadvantaged children, LEP students, and children with various special needs have to go farther to meet the standards. They may fail and be left behind

- National tests mean national curricula. They will inevitably result in the usurpation of educational authority from states and localities and result in greater centralization of control

- Extrapolation from European systems is inappropriate. The United States has greater challenges in the diversity of its student body, no formal policy of early tracking into academic and vocational programs, no nationally centralized curricula, and no recent tradition of a highly regarded teaching profession. European countries have a range of social, health, and family support systems lacking in this country.

- A national assessment system by itself will not result in educational reform on the cheap. Without resources to build the infrastructure we need to improve curriculum, teaching practice, and the quality of teachers going into the schools, we are doomed. And even if we had the national will to make these changes, we don't have the resources to do so.

- Standards are a big step forward, but so far our examples are very generally phrased and may be subject to wide interpretation. We need carefully constructed curricula before we can develop adequate assessment instruments. Specific tests, if created before specific curricula, may drive educational reform in a direction undesired by educational policy makers and repeat previous failures. So we can not do this tomorrow.

- Holding students accountable or requiring certification that has real consequences (for graduation, employment, or opportunity for further education) may be subject to judicial challenge unless school systems can demonstrate that adequate notice of expectations and reasonable opportunity to learn have been provided.

Some negative arguments focus on a system of assessment that would permit individual states or groups of states to develop their own performance assessments of the national standards. Illustrative concerns include:

- Validity studies of performance assessment are just beginning and as yet we do not have strong evidence in support of performance assessment. At this point, they are risky for use for student certification or other high-stakes consequences.

- Fairness of performance assessment results may present problems for two related reasons. First, the evidence to date suggests that it is hard to demonstrate even limited generalizability — that is, successful performance on one task is related to performance on a similar but slightly different task or topic. If different students complete different tasks, assuring the comparability of their results is difficult. Secondly, the effect of comparability of administrative conditions will need to be determined, so as to assure that all children are assessed under standard conditions.

- Performance assessments may prove especially difficult for disadvantaged learners who have not had instructional experiences in extended complex task performance. Evidence (from NAEP) suggests that minority students complete open-ended tasks at a much lower rate. Changing the kind of assessment is no immediate cure-all.

- Performance tasks presently depend substantially on written and oral communication, even in subjects such as science and mathematics. LEP students could be unfairly affected by these tasks. In addition, there may be more opportunities for biases based upon superficial qualities of language (such as a foreign accent or Black English features) to influence judgments.
- The logistics of performance assessment raise questions of practicality. It is not an efficient format; provisions for students not being tested require extra resources if learning is to go on while the testing is in progress.
- The costs of this system in terms of teacher development, task development, administration, scoring, and validation are so high as to be insupportable.

Because the Council has already expressed sentiment against using a single national test, no arguments, although they are numerous, convincing, and strong, will be put forth against that alternative, such as using an individual form of NAEP.

Summary of Arguments

Although it might be desirable, we have not presented counter-arguments and rejoinders to each specific point raised on behalf of or against a new assessment system. How can we summarize the arguments? Some arguments for a national system focus on principles of good management, incentives, and communication. A set of these arguments implies that our failures with assessment and testing in the past can be overcome with new forms of assessments, assessments more closely linked to teaching and focused on valued accomplishments of students. These arguments are essentially optimistic and have relatively little evidence in their support.

Arguments against a national system are based on our past experiences with assessment and on doubts that changes intended by new assessments will actually occur. New, performance based assessments have not as yet accumulated a sufficient track record on validity, reliability, fairness, practicality, and efficiency to permit their wholesale adoption as a national policy for all assessment purposes, and for high-stakes purposes in particular. No single examination has been able simultaneously to serve the purposes of monitoring system progress, student certification, accountability, instructional improvement, and school evaluation as well as maintain the validity of the measure for all its purposes. At minimum, we must consider different assessments for different purposes.

One partial way out of this negativism is to look toward the provision of indicators of school and system capacity as means to both assess the quality of the system and to provide collateral evidence relevant to the validity and fairness of the student performance assessments.

Although most interest and discussion have been devoted to the development of student assessments of the national standards, the adoption of capacity indicators requires a significant commitment of energy as well. To this point, there have been numerous efforts to assess capacity, in terms of resources and educational processes.

Some have been created to report to the public on the status of schools, for instance, School Report Cards that include information both on capacity at the school and on school performance. Some have been used as accountability mechanisms with varying success. Some of these have been cast in the form of educational indicators of inputs, processes, and outputs as means to monitor and explain changes in our educational system. The recent report, *Education Counts*, prepared by the Congressionally mandated study panel on indicators provides a detailed vision of the benefits of an indicator system.

Capacity indicators may provide sources of evidence that will increase our confidence in results on outcomes. But indicators of capacity are not without problems. One limit and consequently a source of tension is how to achieve some comparable level of reporting— from school to school, for instance— without overlooking special and important characteristics or efforts of the school. We also need to keep the level of documentation from being burdensome. Finally, we wish to reduce the likelihood that reporting on capacity will result in explicit regulation and prescription.

How can we proceed? First, we must cut our interest in capacity to the bare but essential minimum. Three attributes of system and school capacity are essential to the interpretation of student assessment. (Depending upon the final character of the system and school capacity indicators, other elements may be added.) The minimal elements are:

- equal opportunity to learn curricula implied by the standards — learning resources, instruction, curriculum, teacher and student assignment;
- specific issues about environments for populations with special needs;
- procedures to avoid test misuse.

Information on these points is essential to determine the validity and fairness for any high-stakes use of assessments.

To summarize our views:

- We all believe we can devise methods to improve the way we monitor our progress toward national goals.
- Most of us believe that we cannot use traditional tests as accountability tools to improve performance.
- We only have partial evidence on the likelihood performance assessments will be successful. We are concerned that changing the form of the assessment will not solve basic problems of inappropriate use and we will need to build a carefully documented set of experiences about practicality, validity, reliability, and costs of their use for different assessment purposes.

Our Vision: Toward a System to Assess the National Standards

We conclude that there is no ready-made examination system available for instant use in the assessment of national standards. None brings together the hopes for assessment and the protection against previous failures. But we recognize that assessment is a critical part of the educational reform process and a desirable and appropriate requirement for public enterprises. We realize that we cannot wait until we have researched, debugged, and resolved every unknown. We must cautiously begin to move now.

We recommend a fundamental redesign of our assessment system — a redesign that can start immediately but will take time and care to come to fruition.

- We support an assessment system that protects children from the harms of test misuse, from unfairness, and from poor quality tests and assessments.
- We support an assessment system that holds schools accountable for providing high quality educational programs and for producing the intellectual accomplishments Americans expect of all of their children.
- We support a system that fosters rather than inhibits creative and demanding teaching.
- We need an assessment system to help us assess our progress toward the National Education Goals, and one that provides understandable information that will help mobilize families, students, educators, and the whole community to rededicate themselves to the cause of learning.

Our strategy is based upon a few basic assumptions:

- No one test or assessment should be asked to serve all the assessment purposes. We need, at this point, a system made up of articulated components, glued together by their adherence to content standards, and serving explicit purposes for assessment.
- There is good in the assessment system that should be retained and expanded. Excellent progress in assessment design by states and localities and by commercial test publishers should be put to use in this new assessment system. Most of these efforts focus on the instructional improvement uses of assessments.
- Sufficient safeguards must be built in to the system to protect children, particularly disadvantaged, LEP, and special populations, from negative consequences of the system while it is being refined. Further, assessment should be extended to areas of particular concern to these groups. For example, it is important to ensure a comprehensive assessment of English language skills for LEP students.

We propose, therefore, the development of a system to assess the national standards which cleaves to the following principles:

- It is always conceived as a part of a larger educational reform effort. Assessment is not adopted as a quick fix.
- It functions as a system — not as a cacophonous set of information that provides little guidance. Performance information will be articulated. There will be coherence among assessed grade levels. There will be relationships between information secured to assess system capacity and system performance. Inappropriate uses of the assessments should be avoided.
- It is developmental. We understand it will evolve and change. We will avoid practices that prematurely freeze new assessments.
- It is empirical. We will invest increasing reliance on its results as we develop experience and evidence of its validity, reliability, and fairness for each use and the consequences flowing from each use.
- It will begin with assessing content knowledge because that is what is technically the most feasible. However, there must be the understanding that students do not learn if they are not interested in the subject matter. Thus, direct assessments of student motivation to learn need to be developed to supplement assessment of knowledge.
- Because of this experimental nature, we want to monitor the impact of the assessments on the educational system. If we are in error, we are committed to changing our policies.
- The assessment system will be practical and economical. It will collect as much information as is needed with minimal disruption of instructional time for valid decisions but no more.

Overall Requirements for an Assessment System to Assess the National Standards

The new assessment system must be designed to ensure that states and local districts have the primary responsibilities for creating and implementing assessments for the purposes of accountability, school evaluation, student certification, reporting to parents, and instructional improvement. Such responsibilities should be state and local because decisions about schooling are made primarily at the state and local levels. Furthermore, there is no single best method of assessment. We need to provide for the creative development of multiple alternatives to assess the national standards.

The responsibility for assuring the quality of these assessments would reside at the national level. The national level would also be responsible for monitoring progress toward the National Goals (this responsibility would be fulfilled by using NAEP, as it is modified to reflect emerging national content standards), additional national responsibilities are independently evaluating the impact of the assessment system on the Nation's educational quality and equity, and providing resources for technical assistance, research, and development on assessment so that the system may be improved.

State and Local Responsibilities

States or groups of states have the responsibility to devise differentiated assessments of the national standards. They may use these different assessments ultimately for purposes of monitoring progress, accountability, student certification, instructional improvement, or school evaluation. For a state to participate in the system to assess national standards, its assessments must meet certain assessment quality standards.

States are to be encouraged to explore wide options in how they approach the design of assessments of the content standards. They are encouraged to develop innovative schedules of administration and improved procedures to report to their publics. There will be many legitimate strategies adopted by states to reach the content standards. Consequently, it is expected that there will be diverse interpretations of these standards in curriculum and teaching practices. This diversity is to be encouraged and is a welcome part of our Nation's educational heritage. But all assessments used as part of the national standards process must be developed to reasonable levels of validity and fairness.

National Responsibilities

There are four responsibilities at the national level:

1) Assuring quality of assessments
2) Monitoring progress toward Goal 3 of the National Education Goals
3) Independent studies of the impact of the assessment system
4) Technical assistance, development, and research

Assuring Quality of Assessments

Assessments must be judged to be consistent with the national standards and to meet criteria of validity, reliability, and fairness. Without this quality assurance at a national level, we have no way of developing a truly national system. Quality standards for the development and use of assessments will be developed and adopted by a nationally authorized entity.

Quality standards for the development and use of assessment will be developed and adopted by a national entity. These quality standards will be adapted as appropriate from the *Standards for Educational and Psychological Testing* (American Educational Research Association, American Psychological Association, National Council on Measurement in Education, 1985) and will also include the eight criteria articulated in the *Criteria for Evaluation of Student Assessment Systems* (National Forum on Assessment, 1991). Such quality standards, incorporated in promulgated guidelines, should be helpful to states and local districts in the development of assessments.

Two principal concerns are to be addressed by this entity: standards of assessment validity and standards of assessment equity.

Standards of Assessment Validity

For assessments to be valid, they minimally must assess the developed content standards. The entity will assure that the assessments proposed by states or groups of states are aligned with the national content standards.

If high-stakes uses of assessment are desired, volunteering states will provide empirical evidence of the validity of their assessments. The entity will review the validity studies to determine if they provide reasonable evidence to support the adoption of such high-stakes uses of assessment. This review and recommendation is necessary but not sufficient for high-stakes use of the results of the assessments.

The entity will create guidelines and conduct studies to determine the comparability of assessments from different states or groups of states. At the outset, guidelines will be promulgated and reviews will relate to the comparability of assessment design, for example, in content quality, challenge to students, and content coverage. As available, empirical studies will be conducted to audit the operational comparability of assessments, standardization of administration, and to report publicly on comparability for given standards.

Standards of Assessment Equity

States will come forward with their plans for assuring equity in assessment design, administration, and use for gender, for special populations, disadvantaged students, and LEP students for review by this entity.

There are three principal concerns regarding equity in assessment of LEP and other student populations:

- If students are not assessed because of the lack of instruments, they will fail to benefit from the presumed desirable effects of assessment (improved instruction, accountability, and targeting of resources).

- If LEP students are assessed in English on subject matters such as mathematics, their performance will be handicapped to varying degrees by their English skills. The problem is not easily resolved even by assessment through the native language because of the heterogeneity of students and instructional programs for LEP students. Special procedures will need to be developed to take language and culture into consideration for appropriate assessment.

- All students must be provided opportunity to learn.

The entity will design in consultation with state and local educators guidelines for the collection of evidence on system and school capacity indicators, with specific attention to equity protection. Decisions will be made related to the differential need for capacity indicators for different assessment purposes. States will provide such evidence as it becomes available. When evidence of both capacity indicators and validity standards is adequate, the entity will support the use of high-stakes assessment with secondary school students. It is anticipated that the entity will conduct audit studies, visiting samples of schools, to verify the capacity and equity evidence provided by states.

Rationale for Assessment Quality Assurance Function

Our assessment system must accommodate to the realities of state and local responsibility for education. The entity provides a technically responsible mechanism for assuring that the assessments are national, and are reasonable interpretations of the standards. Creativity and flexibility of assessments should be encouraged.

Validity evidence for promising new assessments is not fully available and all agree that such evidence must await the design and preliminary use of assessments of the national standards. It is impossible to examine the validity, reliability, and fairness of assessments not as yet produced, but we must responsibly give notice that high standards of assessment will be expected. The national function of assuring the quality of assessments provides this notice.

The entity will assist state or other entities and assist in the preparation of evidence on validity, reliability, fairness, and attention to the needs of special populations of proposed assessments. Validity evidence will be provided for the specific use to be made of the assessment in view of the populations assessed.

Evidence on the quality of system and school capacity indicators will be needed for a number of reasons: 1)to assure quality and comparability of information; 2)to permit reasonable inferences about the operation of the education system nationally; 3)to be used to avoid unintended narrowing of curricula; 4)to provide critical information on opportunity to learn, treatment of special populations, and the avoidance of misuse of assessment before high-stakes assessment is recommended.

Audit or verification through selected school visits is required so that: 1)undue process information is not required of local districts and states; 2)the guidelines for evidence do not inappropriately prescribe instructional or other school or system processes; 3)information is generated to make the capacity assessment more effective and efficient; 4)special policy-relevant information can be obtained for use by the entity, the Standards Council, or Congress. School visits will be made by teams of skilled school practitioners.

The membership of the entity will be primarily technical to fit with their charge. Experts in measurement, assessment, subject matter, learning, classroom processes, and special populations will comprise the entity.

Monitoring System Progress Toward Goal 3 of the National Education Goals

A critical national responsibility is monitoring progress toward the National Education Goals. The most effective and efficient method of monitoring progress toward Goal 3 is the National Assessment of Educational Progress (NAEP). NAEP, with the oversight of the National Assessment Governing Board (NAGB), should continue in its present role. Although development and refinement is necessary for

NAEP to assess the content standards, NAEP is well designed for meeting this monitoring function for the Nation and the states. A broad-based NAEP that provides comprehensive assessments of important subject matter areas is needed to provide independent information about our educational progress. NAEP has a critical role to play in meeting the national responsibility of monitoring progress.

Rationale for an independent NAEP. The monitoring function of NAEP must be preserved and kept separate from the newly redesigned assessment process so as to remain a source of independent evidence on the progress our Nation is making toward attaining its Goals. Importantly, as NAGB has recently noted, NAEP serves as a general check on the trends of educational progress, trends that may not be available from any other source. NAGB must continue to give its full attention to the development and improvement of NAEP to meet simultaneously the need for progress information and the need to adapt as appropriate to the national standards.

Independent Evaluation of the Impact of the Assessment System

The Assessment Task Force considers it essential that independent evaluations of the effects of any national assessment system be conducted on a continuing basis. These evaluations should be the responsibility of one or more organizations that are independent of those that establish the national standards or develop or approve the assessments used in the national assessment system. As a check on the system, the evaluations should examine several different aspects of the assessments. They may investigate independently the reliability and validity of the examinations for specific uses. They should evaluate the fairness of the examinations for various groups of students. In addition, the evaluations should explore the impact of the assessments on learning and the overall quality of the educational system. These studies should have a national focus and have as primary audiences the public, Congress, the Secretary of Education, and the National Education Goals Panel. Evaluations might determine if assessments have had positive impact on the opportunity of students, the quality of instruction, or the confidence of the public in the quality of students' accomplishments. Studies may address negative impact of assessment on equity concerns, curriculum and teaching practices, and on student opportunity to learn.

Technical Assistance, Development, and Research

To assess the National Education Goals, we need "break-the-mold" assessments. If we don't have them, a nagging concern is that innovation will recede to the level of less creative assessments used. We will need a bold and significant program to develop new types of assessments and wish to involve talent from a variety of sources. Substantial Federal financial support should be made available to states and local districts, working in partnership with commercial test publishers, universities and other educational institutions, to develop new assessments that can fulfill the vision of a positive assessment role in educational reform.

An additional national function is to provide technical assistance to states, local school districts, and their teachers to help them profit from the planned value of the assessment system. Specifically, technical assistance must be supported for the design, implementation, staff development, and reporting requirements for new assessments.

Finally, a research program should be supported to help solve problems in design, analysis, and interpretation of new assessments. Areas requiring research will include, among others, new approaches to comparability, generalizability and fairness of assessments, adaptation of assessments to special needs of students, and issues of aggregation and reporting.

All of these functions could be carried out by the United States Department of Education.

Summary on Desirability

Validity, reliability, and equity standards must be built in to any adopted national system. Because we do not have the standards and assessments in front of us to review, we have to create a process to safeguard their quality. A voluntary system of assessment is desirable if the system respects state and local control of education and assures the validity, reliability, and fairness of the assessments.

Recommendations:

• The NAEP should be the mechanism on a matrix-sampled basis to monitor our national progress toward the national standards.

• A national examination system, or system of assessments, based substantially on assessments of the standards by individual states or groups of states, is desirable under certain conditions. Specifically, such assessments should be used for instructional improvement purposes until evidence of their validity for high-stakes purposes is obtained.

• An independent quality assurance "entity" should be created to review the validity, reliability, and fairness of assessments in the new system. For high-stakes uses, volunteering states will provide evidence of their own choice of the validity and fairness of the assessment for the purpose intended.

• A long-term, independent study should be conducted of the impact of any national system of assessment on the quality of education, student accomplishments, and educational equity in the United States.

Feasibility

Feasibility of the assessment system hinges on a variety of factors: enabling conditions, incentives, and costs.

Enabling Conditions

Three enabling conditions are required: the development of standards, the technical know-how to develop such assessments and the infrastructure to support such assessments, including concerns of practicality and logistics.

The development of standards is essential so that early development of appropriate assessments can begin. The development of curriculum is necessary so that assessments can be appropriately integrated into the instructional sequence and so that "opportunity to learn indicators" can be developed and implemented. Whether curricula or assessments need be developed first is a matter of contention and best left up to individual and groups of states to decide.

What is our technical knowledge base to develop valid new assessments? On the one hand, we cannot answer the question literally until we see the standards emerging from consensual subject matter processes. On the other hand, we have a robust and busy community developing and exploring the properties of new assessments. Many are using similar measures to focus learning, to reform the curriculum, and to improve teaching right now. Because we have proposed a developmental process that will reduce the likelihood of premature use of such measures for high-stakes purposes, the feasibility of the system on technical grounds is reasonable, particularly if recommendations are adopted to improve the development, research, and technical assistance bases.

Logistical concerns are many and include a wide range of topics, from making sure teachers understand how administration and scoring techniques relate to instruction to classroom management techniques to allow valid assessment to occur. The practicality of early efforts will need to be examined objectively to avoid negative side effects of a new assessment system.

Incentives

What incentives for participation in assessment development and implementation must be created? An obvious choice is to provide relief from certain Federal and state testing requirements. Logically, we can not imagine simply layering on more assessment to that which is already in place. For example, relief from existing testing requirements could come in the form of encouraging the substitution of new assessments of the standards, perhaps performance assessments or indicators of capacity, for current requirements. These options would serve to free up staff and other resources for engagement in the design of new assessments. "Break-the-mold" assessment development funds could provide a desirable jump-start to the process. Other options would allow commercial publishers of assessment to deduct their research and development costs to permit their investment in new assessment strategies. We suggest that decisions about incentives should be an early agenda item for deliberation by any successor group to the Council.

Costs

The proposed system will require fiscal resources as well as reallocation of the time of teachers and others. By any rough estimate the system will be expensive. Costs will depend upon frequency of assessment tasks, whether scoring is internal or external to the school. Examinations can cost $65 a student for externally administered, multiply scored efforts down to only a few dollars a student. We are estimating grossly we have about 10 million children to be tested annually, if each student were individually measured. Our cost estimates vary directly with the complexity of the effort. Sampling students could vastly reduce costs. Furthermore, the cost of the operation of an entity with an audit or school function is considerable. Rough estimates, based on the Inspectorate system in Great Britain, suggest that costs per school visit range around $25,000. Even if contained by economies of sampling and scheduling, these costs are massive. Furthermore, studies of national impact, technical assistance, and research and development require considerable resources. We would hope the "break-the-mold" assessments would be funded at a level comparable to other major elements of the education reform effort. We are very much in need of credible estimates to be even in the ball park and request that the Council to seek assistance from an entity such as the Congressional Budget Office or findings, if available, from the Office of Technology Assessment study on testing to assist in the accurate estimate of costs for the development and operation of the national and state components. But we can assure the Council it will take considerable resources to fulfill the vision.

Who Pays for It?

State and local governments are not able to support new assessment costs at the same time state economies are in trouble. It is hard to justify costs of assessment as instructional resources constrict. Even if participants in this assessment system were given relief by the Federal and state governments from certain student testing requirements, the funds generated would be relatively small against the need. But we need to find resources for the support of desirable new assessments meeting the standards. Support is essential by the Federal Government for the development of "break-the-mold" assessments by states or groups of states to meet the national standards. The private sector may be helpful, particularly foundations and businesses with interests in improving schools. But their discretionary resources are increasingly limited.

We may also be naive at this time to believe that a complex development process such as we are proposing has to start on all fronts for every child immediately. We may not be able to pay the full bill right now, and we may want to pay as we go. States may very well have to size their efforts to the pocketbook available and pick particular subject matters on which to concentrate. Similarly, they might focus attention on particular localities or districts to permit the process to go forward in the current economic environment.

Similarly, it would be essential to obtain in written testimony opinions of states on the financial trade-offs and their estimated costs to meet quality assurance standards.

Recommendation:

The Assessment Task Force believes it is feasible to develop a system to assess national standards on technical grounds if we adhere to the developmental principles underlying the proposed design particularly the use of differentiated assessments for different purposes. The feasibility of system costs will depend upon what resources are made available by the Federal Government to initiate and sustain the process. The Council may wish to consider cost sensitive and resource leveraging schedules to encourage some activity to begin immediately.

Implementation

We propose taking our lead from the business community and to adopt an implementation strategy that rests on the idea of rapid prototyping — getting something, even something modest, into trials early, and adopting a test-and-fix approach — to improve our assessments as we go. Critical to this overall strategy are three points: coordinating development in a few priority areas, for example mathematics, reading, and writing, for fourth grade; encouraging different strategies and approaches; and reporting descriptive information as early as possible to the public, parents, policymakers, educators, and students.

First Steps Recommended to the Council:
- Encourage the development and trial of assessments of the NCTM standards.
- Make governance decisions, and seek authorization and funding for the National Quality Assurance function.
- Encourage the funding of research projects and new "break-the-mold" assessments.
- Move toward encouraging the relief of certain existing Federal and state testing requirements for participants in the national standards process.

Issues

There arose in the Task Force discussions a number of issues that we wish to acknowledge briefly and bring to the Council's attention. They are not integrated into the body of the desirability and feasibility discussion because they may be regarded as beyond our charge. But we believe their consideration will ultimately impact the quality of any implemented assessment system. One major concern is the narrow focus on the five subject matters identified in the legislation. We are aware that the Goal 3 language is broader, and that the report in *Education Counts* of the special indicators panel also recommends a broad based consideration of outcomes. Particularly of interest are outcomes that integrate across learning disciplines and that focus on skills that underlie many different kinds of performances. Attitudes, dispositions, and engagement are also important. One obvious area that is missing from our explicit consideration, although mentioned repeatedly in our discussion, is how to deal with the recommendations of the Department of Labor's commission on workforce skills (Secretary's Commission on Achieving Necessary Skills (SCANS)).

Expanding the foci for assessment is valuable because it provides choices to students of the areas in which they wish to focus. For instance, in many European countries students may choose among a variety of areas, including the arts, foreign languages, and somewhat more practical fields. Notwithstanding the cost constraints described above, we believe that a system that provides opportunity for students to emphasize at least in part their special talents and goals is the sort of system we should strive for. Clearly, this is a *prior* matter for the consideration of the group charged with content standards.

Discussions among the Task Force members also dealt with governance issues: who funds, manages, and insulates the quality assurance functions described. Different positions were strongly held, and we believe there are a range of arguments to be made on their behalf.

A persistent concern was, of course, that even our minimalist system would be too costly or complex, and that the outcome and high-stakes features of the system would dominate the process. We believe that standards of validity, reliability and fairness, as well as concerns for special populations will not be served without the minimum components that we have proposed.

Summary

We recommend to the Council that they support the desirability of a system to assess the national standards as proposed. This system separates purposes of assessment, supports responsibility for design, development, implementation and public reporting of assessments at the state and local level, and provides for a set of essential national functions. State roles in this assessment system assure that appropriate traditions for the local responsibility for education will be observed.

A major national function is quality assurance of the assessments. Quality is assured in terms of adherence to the national standards, and validity of assessments used for various purposes and student groups. Particularly important are the indicators of opportunity to learn, equity provisions for special populations, and the avoidance of the misuse of assessments. School visits to verify capacity evidence will be conducted on a sampling basis in the service of improving the process. The quality assurance function would also be responsible for developing reports on the comparability of measures developed by the various individual or groups of states.

Another critical national function is the continuation of the independent role of NAEP as a mechanism to monitor national progress toward goals. Strong consensus exists to preserve the credibility of NAEP and the provision of trend information as it moves toward assessment of the national standards.

Similarly it is an essential national function to evaluate the effects of this proposed system. Our requirements provide that we immediately implement long-term studies of impact on the education system and on our students of any newly designed assessment system.

A program of "break-the-mold" assessments is proposed to provide additional momentum to the system plan in order to improve its chances of success.

Finally, programs to provide needed technical assistance and continued research to address emerging technical problems should be supported.

The Task Force considered feasibility and believes that the system is feasible technically if developmental and validity principles are upheld in the quality assurance process. The Council needs reliable cost figures for the development and operation of the assessment system. Particularly, early steps were suggested to get this system launched immediately.

Raising Standards for American Education

Report of the Implementation Task Force

The National Council on Education Standards and Testing was established to provide advice regarding the desirability and feasibility of national standards, a national examination system, and related issues. Underlying the interest in standards and assessment is deep concern arising from persistent evidence that the academic prowess of American students is seriously deficient. This deficiency touches all student groups regardless of income, race, language, gender, or disability. Thus, Congress is interested in high standards and rich assessment strategies for all students. At the same time, a number of questions posed by the Congress to the Council concerning "wide variations in resources available to school systems," the special challenge of success posed by "economically disadvantaged children, handicapped children, and children with limited English proficiency," the use of national examinations "for unintended purposes (such as sorting and tracking of students)," and "whether... it is feasible... to challenge all children to do their best without penalizing those of lesser educational opportunity" make it clear that equity is a central issue to the Congress. The Task Force shares that equity concern.

Neither the Congress nor the Council is interested in simply creating higher standards and new tests so that the Nation can know one more time that our students perform poorly. Significant improvement in performance by all students, including those with whom we historically fail, is the objective. The Council is clear that

The views expressed in this appendix report reflect the work of this Task Force and are not necessarily those of the Council.

simply creating higher standards and new tests will not result in significant improvement. The Implementation Task Force was created by the Council to offer advice to the Council as to what must be done to ensure that most students are able to demonstrate on the rich new assessment strategies they know and can do what the new higher standards will call for. Absent leadership in helping students achieve, the standards and assessments, as the Standards Task Force has said, will be a cruel hoax.

Our report[7], therefore, is based on the following assumptions: (1)all students can learn at significantly higher levels; (2)academic achievement must increase dramatically in English, mathematics, science, history, and geography if the Nation is to maintain its economic strength and democratic institutions; (3)increases in achievement must be demonstrated by youngsters with whom we historically fail — the poor, disabled, and language minority — as well as with students with whom we have been relatively more successful; (4)marginal changes in schools of the reform character practiced for the past decade will continue to yield mediocre results with virtually all students; (5)there are many reports of potentially promising practices, but there is little knowledge about how to be successful with students on a large scale; (6)we should rethink how present funds are being invested in education and not hesitate to incorporate more cost effective practices when appropriate; and (7)substantial additional resources will be necessary, but "more of the same" is not enough. Any increased spending must purchase measurably productive change.

These assumptions lead us to the conclusion that only deep and systemic change will have the power to alter school, district, state, and community behavior sufficiently for virtually all students to meet the new standards the Nation requires. The depth and breadth of necessary change will involve a number of integrated parts. The integrated and comprehensive character of what we propose cannot be overemphasized. The piecemeal, project-oriented, narrowly focused mentality that has affected much of the largely failed reform measures to date must give way to broader strategies that are connected vertically (school, district, state, Nation) and horizontally (within a school, district, state, Nation). The Congress called on the Council to determine the desirability of national standards and assessments. National standards and assessments are not desirable without comprehensive initiatives such as those suggested below.

High standards and assessment strategies rich enough to measure the extent to which students have met them are our reference points. By high standards, we have in mind the knowledge, understanding, and application of complex facts and processes; the ability to conceive, infer, and deduce ideas and reach conclusions; the capacity

---

7. Three documents made a special contribution to our thinking. They are: (1) *Educating America*, a report from the NGA that identified implementation activities they thought would be important to achieve the national goals; (2) "Systemic School Reform" (*Politics of Education Association Yearbook 1990*, 233-267), a paper by Marshall S. Smith and Jennifer O'Day, setting forth elements of systemic efforts underway across the country and thoughts about the key factors that must be addressed; and (3) *The Essential Components of a Successful Education System*, which is the public policy agenda of The Business Roundtable.

to communicate effectively; and the skill to work productively with others. We believe such knowledge and capacity to perform will be reflected in the full range of disciplines embodied in the humanities, mathematics, and sciences. Rich assessment strategies are those that can measure the type of standards reflected in those examples. They will likely include portfolios, projects, and performance-based strategies. Some will involve individuals demonstrating competence at a particular point in time. Others may involve activities performed by groups of students over a period of time. We have paused to describe the character of standards and assessment that governed our thinking to make the point that we believe it is those kinds of standards and assessment that are desirable if schools, districts, states and the Nation provide the support that will enable students to meet the standards.

The equitable implementation of high standards and rich assessment strategies depends on well-prepared teachers and administrators, equipped with proper tools. The tools include curriculum resources, instructional approaches, and technologies that will enable children of diverse backgrounds and interests to achieve the national standards. Teachers and administrators need the support of governance systems that are efficient and helpful, not top-heavy and inhibiting. They must be provided strong support from the non-school community. They must function within a system that places a premium on student outcomes and professional practice. Since students spend far more of their lives out of school than inside, achievement of standards will depend on building of communities of and for children and parents that support the health and well-being of youngsters that are a precondition of learning.

We will, therefore, discuss implementation within eight broad categories:

- Curriculum resources and instructional strategies
- Incentives
- Governance system
- Staff capacity
- Support systems for students and their families
- Technology
- Public understanding and support
- Equity

Curriculum Resources and Instructional Strategies

Curriculum resources and instructional strategies need not (indeed, should not) be separate from assessment as routinely as is presently the case. The lines between instruction and assessment must be blurred both from the curriculum and the assessment perspective. We advocate assessment strategies that will make "teaching to the test" desirable. It should also be noted that for curriculum and instructional strategies to make sense to teachers, the teachers must be engaged in both developing curriculum frameworks and in identifying the characteristics that distinguish resources and strategies likely to help students achieve the national standards from those that will not. While we address the development of staff capacity below, we note here that opportunity for teachers to work with and develop curriculum on site will play a very important role in a staff having the ability to teach effectively.

The definition of national standards must include the crafting of state curriculum frameworks. Such frameworks will make clear that we must abandon the minimum skill orientation, the emphasis on coverage not depth of understanding, and the premium that is often placed on students knowing isolated facts. Instead, the curriculum frameworks will be discipline-based, oriented toward thinking, understanding, problem solving, and knowledge integration with connections to the real world. Such frameworks should provide parameters, not prescriptions, for practice. It is necessary to provide the school staff with access to the tools of teaching and learning, the curriculum resources, and the capacity to identify or develop good instruction strategies, including interactive technologies.

For curriculum materials and strategies to be outstanding, they must be linked to the standards and assessment strategies on which the Council is focused. A process must be put in motion to develop characteristics of curriculum resources and instructional strategies likely to help all students achieve the national standards, without it resulting in a one-size-fits-all mentality. Examples might include: (a)- the depth of the material; (b)the richness of recommended class exercises; and (c)how much emphasis is placed on student dialogue, cooperative learning, and writing. We believe this process should also include the next step of having an appropriate authority actually review curriculum material and other instructional resources against the characteristics. The appropriate authority could be the state or, perhaps, a consortium of states and cities, working with professional and discipline-based associations from which the standards and assessment strategies may emerge. It is important that this review process be rigorous. Absent special attention to rigor, it would likely result in the lowest common denominator of curriculum material in an effort to minimize controversy and increase sales. A process for extending a meaningful "Good Housekeeping Seal" to assist in the voluntary identification and adoption of good practice would then be possible. To avoid the image that good practices are readily transportable across very different contexts, the "Seal" process could be accompanied by carefully documented reports of practices that were apparently successful (or problematic) in specific settings.

Incentives

A key component of any outcome-driven systemic change strategy is that consequences must be attached to the performance of staff in the schools and at the district level and to the performance of students. Intrinsic factors play an extremely important role in motivating people. The sense of "a job well done" or the satisfaction of helping a student achieve extraordinary goals or another student to turn his life around are the types of factors that lead most educators to teach in the first place. Moreover, good working conditions, district and community support, and acknowledgment of good effort are also significant. But it is clear that extrinsic factors also play a role in shaping how and how hard people work — staff and students alike. While incentives, positive and negative, are not sufficient to move the system — high standards, rich assessment, changes in governance, professional development, health and social service support, technology, and more time for teachers and at least some students are also necessary — incentives are an essential component.

Staff of Schools and Districts

In designing a strong incentive system for schools or school districts, there are a number of principles we believe deserve consideration.

Incentives need to be tied directly to achievement of high standards related to both student outcomes and professional practice. We contrast this with the widespread present practice of encouraging focus almost exclusively on inputs (filling out forms) and low-level skills (minimum competency tests).

Incentives for school and district staff need to be powerful enough to rivet staff attention on the achievement of the high standards.

Incentives should place a premium on doing better with students with whom we presently do the poorest job as well as those with whom we do the best. It is very important that we have learning environments in which all students dramatically move up the achievement continuum from where they presently are. We contrast this with present incentive systems, for example, that encourage experienced teachers to work with the least challenging students or lead to "pushing out" the most challenging students or to encourage the absence of the poorest students on days assessment is to occur or to retain in grade the most difficult youngsters.

Incentives should be designed to reward value added by a school over a defined period of time. We contrast this with focusing on inter-school comparisons, which tend to measure demographic characteristics more than the difference a school is making in the achievement of students.

Incentive systems should be designed so that students are not harmed. For example, if penalties are a part of the incentive system, financial penalties or even dismissal for persistently failing staff, at the district and school level may be appropriate but not the withdrawal of funds for the school program itself. Indeed, it may be appropriate for such schools to have more program funds, not less.

There should be a spectrum of incentives. The positive end should include such things as financial rewards for staff at both the district and school levels, opportunities to participate in special professional development, and recognition programs. Schools experiencing difficulty should be assisted through technical assistance, extra professional development and special funding. Staff in schools and school districts persistently failing could face penalties including public disclosure, loss of students, staff financial loss, dismissal of staff and school reorganization.

There is no one best way to design an incentive system. Moreover, a single approach will likely not work forever. Incentives are situational and can be tricky to implement without causing unintended results. These words of caution are intended to encourage thoughtfulness and sophistication in the design of the system, recognizing that an over-simplistic or crude system rooted in a punishment focus would be counterproductive.

Students

There are a number of considerations related to providing incentives for students to work harder. They include:

- At the present time, except for those applying to the most competitive four-year colleges in the United States, most high-school graduates are admitted to the college of their choice. Thus, most students know there is not much "pay off" related to higher education for outstanding performance. Systems of collaboration with post secondary education institutions of all kinds should be designed to make clear to students that elementary/secondary performance influences post-secondary education opportunities.
- Quality alternatives to college for the "forgotten half," such as apprenticeship programs, which also require strong entry skills, need to be developed in partnership with the business and labor communities.
- Systems of collaboration with employers should be designed to make clear to students that elementary/secondary performance influences hiring decisions. In designing the systems, special care must be taken to prevent such standards from being used in a fashion that would result in undesirable behavior such as racial discrimination.
- A variety of incentives short of jobs and post-secondary training/education opportunities that encourage hard work by students should be considered. They could, of course, include traditional factors such as grades. In addition, students could be given greater choice of learning opportunities, choice of projects, working in groups, etc.
- High stakes for students should follow high stakes for schools. If we have high standards, rigorously maintained, we must give schools time to learn to succeed with increasing proportions of students school-wide before we penalize individual students. Otherwise, students will again bear the full brunt of the system's failure.

Governance system

We believe the systemic change that is necessary to have all youngsters achieve the new high standards will involve new roles and relationships for the participants. Principles that govern these new roles and relationships should include the following.

- In the exercise of power, authority and responsibility should be held in parallel. If more responsibility for student performance is moved down the bureaucratic pipeline, more authority and the resources associated with that authority should follow or vice versa. Power and authority should be exercised as close to the individual student as is consistent with effective accountability.

- Each level of government should examine its standards and regulations in order to remove any that are or are perceived to be an impediment to appropriate decisions at lower levels.

- Legislative bodies (including Congress, state legislatures, state boards of education, municipal legislative bodies and school boards) and non-educator executives (including the President, governors, and mayors) should be decisively involved in goal and curriculum standards determination (outcome definition), policy decisions related to the nature of assessments, a determination of consequences to be attached to student outcome performance, and the provision of adequate and equitably distributed resources. Education management and school-based personnel should then be given the freedom to get the job done within a period of time that has been agreed upon.

- Each level of government should address the adequacy and equitable distribution of resources in levels below it to ensure at least equity of opportunity of all students to reach the high standards we envision. For the federal government, for example, that means attention to initiatives such a ESEA Chapter I, Head Start, and Education for the Handicapped Act. For states and districts, this principle includes elimination of the present widespread fiscal inadequacy and inequity between districts and, within districts, between schools.

- The governance structure should be a function of what works. Radically different models of governance are possible in the public sector. For example, charter schools; charter districts operated within a public utility concept; school-based shared decision-making; boards of children and families that collapse distinctions among education, health, and social service agencies; and children's welfare boards are among governance proposals that have been made in the hope of contributing to higher achievement of students.

Staff Capacity

This area is extraordinarily important. We are asking schools to accomplish levels of achievement that have never been accomplished. We are asking that the diversity of students achieving at those high levels be broader than ever before. The nature of the expected learning for the majority of students — thinking, problem solving, integration of knowledge, working in teams — is different. The nature of assessment will be different. The locus of decision-making will be different. Pedagogy, with greater reliance on strategies such as dialogue, writing, and community based experiences, will be different. The tools of teaching and learning technology will be different. In short, a radically different kind of teaching will be required of most teachers. To do what must be done will require time for staff and exceptionally hard intellectual work. With changes so wide and deep, the professional development of staff is central. The radically different behavior on many fronts will not occur by passing a law or issuing directives. Major changes will be required both before and after the commencement of service as teachers and administrators.

Pre-Service Professional Development

Pre-service education should be linked to the national standards and prepare teachers with the knowledge and skills to help diverse students to achieve the standards. But this is difficult. Pre-service teacher education has undergone little change over the years. Present training in neither content nor in pedagogy is adequate. As teachers come into the profession, they require a broad and deep knowledge of their subject matter. This poses a particularly strong challenge to colleges of arts and sciences since it is there and not in colleges of education where content is most often addressed. This, for example, may require, for elementary teachers especially, a concentration in math/science or humanities instead of the once-over-lightly approach to everything. While ultimate teaching competence will be honed in practice, strong pedagogical pre-service education is also important. If we are to change from a model of teacher as the worker and deliverer of knowledge with the students as passive receptacle to a model of teacher as coach and facilitator and student as worker, it will require very different pre-service preparation.

If we are to have significantly better teachers entering the profession, it will likely involve strategies such as a rigorous and carefully developed performance-based assessment for entry level teachers based on standards directly linked to the national standards for students. All teachers, whether they enter teaching through a traditional or alternate route, should be expected to meet high standards of subject matter knowledge and pedagogical skill. Change in pre-service preparation will be impeded unless accrediting bodies and program standard-setting institutions such as the National Council for the Accreditation of Teacher Education and the National Association of State Directors of Teacher Education change their standards to coordinate with the new national student standards. Their standards need to be made consistent with the teaching standards being developed by the National Board for Professional Teaching Standards (NBPTS).

In-Service Human Resources Development

Most of the teachers presently teaching were not trained to function with the new necessary capacities. They have not taught in schools where such behavior is exhibited. They have not had role models of such teaching to emulate. There is no reason to expect most to have the capacities required to have all students meet the new standards. Most of the present teachers will be in the teaching force for a long time. Thus, a far-reaching in-service human resources development initiative is vital if we want students to achieve the new standards. We underscore the following principles:

• Effective professional development must be defined specifically in relationship to what students need to know or be able to do (national standards). It needs to be sustained, intense, and targeted on both discipline-based and pedagogical content and on instructional tools such as technology related to the teacher's job. In the private sector, when new corporate goals, products, or technologies are introduced, companies organize the time of workers so needed re-education and training can be pursued as part of the worker's regular work responsibilities, whether the additional training occurs on-site or off-site. Similarly, when changes in teachers' responsibilities occur because of new educational goals, new forms of evaluation, new kinds of students, new curricula, or new technologies, professional development must be offered in the context of the teacher's job, not as an "add-on" on weekends or after school.

• The best professional development will be done in school as, for example, teachers work on curriculum development, create assessment tasks, and learn from their peers. Such activities should be undertaken purposefully as a structured effort to enhance professional capacity. As a corollary to such site-based work, new models of human resources development such as teaching academies or other professional development school models should be encouraged.

Determining what standards define what experienced teachers should know and be able to do and developing the assessment strategies that permit us to know teachers have met the standards are important corollaries to setting student standards and assessment. The NBPTS has embarked on that critical and ambitious effort related to experienced teachers and deserves strong support at all levels of government. Their work, of course, can also inform standard-setting of new teachers recommended above and standard-setting for students.

The training and nurture of superintendents, principals, and others in leadership positions is important since they play such an important role in creating the climate within which learning takes place (or doesn't). Thus, we need to focus on high-performance management qualities such as sharing power, focusing on the well-being of the student, being aware of community/consumer needs, opening lines of communication with staff and parents, and developing strong ties to other public and private non-profit support groups.

Two final comments related to staff capacity must be made. First, it is clear that we must have higher entrance standards into teaching. Standards for staying in must also be more rigorous. In short, it will be tougher to become and remain a teacher in a system committed to high student achievement. Doing the job will also be much different, and maybe even harder, work. As a consequence, fundamental changes in compensation systems, work organizations, and in working conditions are required if we hope to attract and hold sufficient quantities of the quality of people we want teaching and administering.

Second, the issues of adequacy and equitable distribution of resources are particularly important in relationship to staff capacity. Additional time must be provided if professional development is to be part of, not an add-on to, the teacher's job. That costs money. In the districts in which low income, limited-English speaking, and disabled students are disproportionately concentrated, the resources issue as it relates to high standards for teachers and administrators, compensation, work organization, and working conditions is particularly critical.

Support Systems for Students and Their Families

Education does not start in kindergarten or at the first grade, but much earlier. Educators are not a student's first or only teachers. Parents and others in the community fill those roles. Hungry, unhealthy, and homeless children are not going to learn to think critically, solve problems, or otherwise meet the high standards the Council has in mind. It has been estimated that more than 90% of a student's life occurs outside the school. Such facts make it clear that strong leadership, courageous initiatives, and adequate resources directed toward the well-being of students outside the schoolhouse door are necessary to achieve the standards to which we aspire inside the schoolhouse. There are at least three general areas in which action is important.

Parents and Other Student Advocates

Every child requires an advocate. The advocate of choice is the parent. There are several key connections between home and school:

- Parents should support the high expectations reflected in the rigorous standards we anticipate for their children and create the environment at home that demonstrates the premium placed on education (e.g., control distractions such as video games, television, and radio; read to the child; do personal reading; and insist on school attendance).

- Schools should appropriately integrate parents and other resources in the community into the education program itself, not simply use them around the edges in busy work.

- Parent education is important. This includes helping young parents know how to parent. It also can mean the school strengthening the academic skills of the parent. All of this is directed toward helping the parent help the children.

- Schools should communicate with parents, be responsive to them, and involve and work with them to ensure the child's success.

- Many, and increasing numbers of, children do not have a functioning parent or source of similar support. An alternative must be found in those circumstances. On the one hand, we can help strengthen the family and the parent's role in the child's education. Still, when there is not an effective parent, that must not become the school's excuse for failure. There are at least two generic alternative categories. One is what some call home-based guidance. In this context, one version is for all of the staff in a school to undertake some measure of extra oversight and concern for individual children. The other approach (not mutually exclusive) is to assure the support of a trained community-based role model (a mentor, big brother, big sister, etc.) for every youngster needing one.

Early Childhood Education

The evidence is very strong that a quality, developmentally appropriate pre-kindergarten program for disadvantaged students reduces significantly many of the problems associated with poverty. It contributes, therefore, to the degree to which low-income youngsters ultimately may achieve at high levels. We give emphasis to the importance of the program's quality and developmental appropriateness.

Since such programs are less expensive and more effective for children than waiting to provide remediation to them when they are older, at least every disadvantaged student should have the opportunity of participation. In order to assure the opportunity for all, it may be wise to consider providing for all and making it free for low income students. Such an approach would avoid the effort being perceived as a poverty program. It could also contribute to racial and economic integration.

It is also clear that such early childhood programs are most effective when continuing support for the students is provided through elementary school to prevent backsliding.

Health and Social Services

Students whose most elemental shelter, food, and nurturing needs are not met are not going to perform at the minimum competency level consistently, much less demonstrate they meet world-class academic standards. The health and social service systems must be restructured to better meet the needs of the poor and the working poor. The coverage of demonstrably effective programs such as prenatal care; Women, Infants, and Children; Early Periodic Screening and Diagnostic Treatment; and the school breakfast and lunch programs must be expanded to cover all children in need.

We recognize that most of the effort necessary to provide health and social service support to children and their families will not be provided by the education system. However, we include it as part of the necessary systems change in our report since it is clear that we will not achieve high national standards with a large proportion of American children, absent change in the other systems. Indeed it may be necessary at all levels of government to restructure the health and social service systems by employing the same principles we are suggesting for education; for example, identify appropriate outcomes (standards) for which the system will be accountable, develop any necessary assessment strategies, associate consequences for staff with the achievement of outcomes, provide the type of necessary training including cross-system training, alter governance and financing formulae to at least encourage if not force service integration, and provide resources such as adequate health insurance so that all children and families are covered.

Technology

A much greater use of technology will be vital to our goal of having all students achieve the new high standards in at least three ways.

- Technology can enhance instruction when teachers use it as a tool. It permits students to structure complicated efforts. It can promote both the individualization of learning and working in teams. Since much higher level learning occurs best when it arises from "doing the learning" and since video and computer technologies can depict and/or simulate real life, there is much greater opportunity for authentic learning. Multiple technologies permit access to many more dimensions of experience arising from history or science or existence halfway around the globe. A resource-rich environment can be provided in any school anywhere through technology. In this context, the development of software powerfully aligned to the national standards is important. In addition, instruction-related assessment strategies may be powerfully enhanced by technology.

- Technology enhances access in several ways. One is through distance learning. Students can connect to one another (student to student, country to country). Students can connect to sources and levels of knowledge otherwise unavailable (data bases, interactive courses led by scholars, educational television, etc.) Technology can bring to every teacher resources now available only to a privileged few. Two-way video and audio technologies, for example, allow higher education faculty and elementary/secondary faculty to confer in ways that can facilitate training, use of resources, and access to research. The more teachers learn from one another and in ways directly connected to their school and classroom, the more powerful the learning experience. Technology can help make that happen.

  Another perspective on access relates to disabled youngsters. Some technologies make relatively esoteric contributions (providing a speechless child a voice with a voice synthesizer); other helpful technology is routine (off-the-shelf work processing for the learning disabled child).

- Technology is also important in managing data. It can schedule our buses. It can collect and organize student data to help teachers help students. It can reduce administrative overload and permit greater concentration of scarce resources at the school and classroom level.

If we are to use technology in the rich ways suggested above, professional development is crucial. Absent an intense, substantive, sustained, targeted professional development effort that is task based, technology either will not be used or it will simply be used to reinforce present practices such as when it is devoted to drill and practice.

If we are to realize the power of technology, we must enable every school and student to use the most sophisticated technology available to any school and student. This is, of course, a major equity issue as we bring "America on Line" for all, including schools with a concentration of disadvantaged, disabled, and language minority students.

Public Understanding and Support

Less than 25% of the electorate has children in school. There are increasingly more older Americans than young. Most citizens believe the schools in general are in bad shape but that their local school is in good shape. Colleges and employers think the school's product is poor, while the students and their parents think the students are doing pretty well. Most people, including many educators, do not really believe all students can learn. Many parents believe that somebody's child needs to know math and science, but not theirs since the parents functioned just fine without the knowledge. Many do not understand that failing children create "tough luck" for all of us, not just for the failing children. Many believe that the traditional methods of schooling, curriculum, modes of testing, etc., are "correct" since those traditional methods conform to their own experience. Such facts pose a huge communications challenge. They must change if the necessary supportive environment is to be created within which all students will meet the new standards.

We must be clear who has a stake in American children meeting high standards and precisely what the stake is. Parents, educators, the business community, the media, and elected officials must "buy in" to the new standards, new assessments, and initiatives of the kind addressed in this report if the climate is to exist to get the job done. It will be necessary to organize the message block by block, community by community; the print and electronic media must be used effectively; business, religious organizations, unions, and other institutions with regular access to large numbers of people — employees and members — must be engaged in the effort.

In short, the attainment of high standards, as determined by rich assessments, is not the job of schools alone and will not be achieved by schools alone. A critical mass of the citizenry must understand the challenge and, in effect, insist that it be achieved.

Equity

Nothing we have said is worthwhile unless it is built in a manner that moves toward equitable results. Given our demography, the increasing proportions of students with whom we historically fail (about one third of all American students are poor, disabled, or do not speak English as a first language), and the economic and civic needs of the Nation, it has become improved results, not simply the availability of opportunity defined by input regulations, around which the Nation's future revolves. Providing genuine opportunity to all remains a moral imperative. Actually moving significantly toward achieving much higher results by each student than he/she presently exhibits is the Nation's economic imperative. The moral imperative has always confronted us. For the first time in American history, we face the economic imperative of greater equity in outcomes.

Equity will require courage and uncommon action. Examples include fiscal equity (not just equality) within (and, perhaps ultimately, among) states. Another good example of effective action could include major changes in Chapter I of the Elementary and Secondary Education Act when it is reauthorized in 1993 so it embraces the spirit of issues raised in this report (including the use of the national standards and assessments and full funding).

We take the opportunity in this section to emphasize the recommendations in previous sections related to equity. Equity is not something that is, different from or stands outside other issues. It must be integral to every component of a successful education system.

Conclusion

It is important to note that the issues we raise are not issues simply considered seriatim. They are not a menu from which one picks and chooses. Systemic change is by definition comprehensive and integrated. There is a critical mass of change that must occur in the right order with adequate, equitably distributed resources to produce enough synergistic power to move the education system as far as it must move to produce the results on which the Nation's future will be built.

Report of the English Task Force

Background

The English Task Force was created by the National Council on Education Standards and Testing to advise it on the desirability and feasibility of national standards for students in English and language arts. Other task forces were similarly created to advise the Council on standard-setting and assessment in five core subjects: English, mathematics, science, history, and geography. The English Task Force decided to rename itself the English/Language Arts Task Force in order to better reflect the broad range of skills commonly expected to be included in this subject (i.e., reading, writing, speaking, and listening).

Status of Efforts to Develop National Standards in English

There do not already exist nationally accepted standards in English/Language Arts for what should be taught, how it should be taught, or what students should know and be able to do. The National Assessment of Educational Progress (NAEP) has developed reading and writing curriculum frameworks through a national consensus process which are to be used in designing those parts of the 1994 NAEP assessment. The National Council of Teachers of English (NCTE) is currently seeking funds to develop teaching standards, but

The views expressed in this appendix report reflect the work of this Task Force and are not necessarily those of the Council.

the effort is still in the planning stage. Several states, including California, Pennsylvania and others, have developed curriculum frameworks for English/Language Arts and are attempting to align their assessments accordingly. It is important that any national standard-setting process take into account these various important efforts.

Are National Standards Desirable, Given the Wide Range of Student Performance?

National standards can do much to address those wide variations in student performance. They can help ensure access — for all children, regardless of race or background — to a high quality education in English/Language Arts.

Of course, there is a potential for misuse of the standards as well as assessment results. The focus must be on improving education, not sorting and tracking students. Student performance should be viewed on a continuum leading to full subject mastery, with students progressing at the pace that best suits them. Though the Task Force did not attempt to deal with the question of how second language learners will fit in with respect to English/Language Arts standards, it did agree that this issue is an important one that will eventually require careful attention.

What Should Be the Process for Developing New Standards, and How Long Will It Take?

The National Council of Teachers of English (NCTE) and the International Reading Association (IRA) are the major teacher professional groups in this area, and it is important that they be a part of the process. Development of standards in English/Language Arts, however, should also involve educators in other subjects or fields as well as interested lay persons, including business representatives, elected officials, and other policymakers.

Content standards, performance standards, and teaching standards all need to be created. Content standards should be decided on first, beginning with what we want students to know and be able to do at grade 12 (the "product"), then working down through the early grades to establish reasonable benchmarks toward that goal. The content standards should be roughly the same at grades 4, 8, and 12, but the sophistication expected should increase at the upper levels. Performance standards and assessment should be developed in concert, based on the content standards. Examinations are likely to be ready in order of simplicity, with the earlier grades first.

A small number of writers — about three — should actually draft the standards, and a broadly representative group numbering approximately two dozen should review their work. The broader group should meet at roughly one month intervals, providing input and advice on successive drafts. Assuming adequate resources (between $600,000 and $1,000,000) and committed personnel, this intensive process should last about six months. The resulting standards will require continued fine-tuning over time.

Literature is the content specific to the English/Language Arts curriculum and enriches the life experience of all of us. All students—

regardless of race, gender, or background — should be able to recognize a wide variety of great works of literature (appropriate to their grade) and respond thoughtfully and knowledgeably given some choice of topic. The difficulty many students encounter today when they are first introduced to literature in the upper grades is a result of their often minimal exposure at the early and even middle grades; disadvantaged students are typically the ones most deprived of a rich curriculum.

Teaching standards should also be developed to provide suggestions and examples to teachers on helping their students reach the new standards. Teachers should be free, however, to use their professional experience and discretion.

Standards for the broader community, perhaps even including the media, may be something worth considering as well.

Assessing the New Standards

It is important that students be able to demonstrate higher order competence in English/Language Arts skills on a variety of topics. It is vital, therefore, that the standards developed for these skills in English/Language Arts inform those relevant aspects of assessment in other subjects. For example, grading of an essay on a topic in history should apply the appropriate criteria for writing skill as an essay analyzing a poem.

The examination system should have a local component, such as portfolios or teacher evaluations, in addition to the national component. Experimentation should be encouraged in the local (or regional) section.

The resulting examination system should not be yet an another "test" to which students are subjected; it should, instead, replace the outmoded standardized tests many students currently take. And it should be tightly aligned with exemplary classroom practices so that it validates superior teaching and learning.

Meeting the New Standards

Schools and teachers are not currently prepared for a challenging curriculum in English. Substantial attention to re-training of today's teachers will be required, as well as a reexamination of pre-service preparation for future teachers. Other systemic changes, as well as communities serious about the importance of schooling, will be necessary as well.

Report of the Mathematics Task Force

Background

The Task Force on Mathematics is one of eight task forces created by the National Council on Education Standards and Testing to advise it on mathematics standard-setting and assessment. The Council's charge is to report to the Congress, the President, and the American people on the desirability and feasibility of creating national standards in five core subjects (English, mathematics, science, history, and geography), as well as the desirability and feasibility of an examinations system to measure student progress toward the standards.

Status of Efforts to Develop National Standards in Mathematics

The *Curriculum and Evaluation Standards for School Mathematics,* by the National Council for Teachers of Mathematics (NCTM), should be accepted as appropriate "content standards" in mathematics. Though several states are in the process of developing performance standards and assessments in accordance with the NCTM *Standards* (such as California, Indiana, Texas, and Kentucky), these efforts have not so far resulted in a set of performance standards that are widely accepted as authoritative. (The Mathematics Task Force did not find the suggested distinction

---

The views expressed in this appendix report reflect the work of this Task Force and are not necessarily those of the Council.

between "achievement" and "performance" standards a useful one, and this report only uses the term "performance standards".)

Are National Standards Desirable, Given the Wide Range of Student Performance?

The creation of a single set of high-quality math standards for all students — and a national examination system to assess results — is vital in raising the overall poor level of mathematical understanding, and is especially important precisely because of the wide variations in student performance. Every student, regardless of race, gender or background, should be assured quality mathematics instruction in an atmosphere of high expectations for all.

The standards should be created in light of the highest world standards, as well as our own judgement of what is important for students to know and be able to do. No compromises should be made to today's low levels of performance.

Though there should be one set of standards for all, we may wish to allow students to specialize in applying the standards to a particular area of interest. This option must be explored with care, to ensure that no student is limited by a "watered down" curriculum.

To ensure equity, examination results should be reported in conjunction with socio-economic information on those assessed (similar to the current reporting of NAEP scores). Assessment tasks will have to be carefully designed in order to be comprehensible to students from diverse cultural backgrounds. Arrangements should also be made to provide handicapped students a fair opportunity to succeed on the examinations.

What Should Be the Process for Developing the New Standards, and How Long Will It Take?

NCTM should play the key role in coordinating development of the standards. NCTM's content standards will have to be elaborated for grades 4, 8, and 12. The development of meaningful performance standards and assessments requires a multi-phase approach. An iterative process should be employed, involving successive standards drafts and input at each stage from other mathematics professional groups, classroom teachers, and the public. The creation of sample assessment tasks is an integral part of the setting of performance standards and must be done in parallel. A variety of sample tasks will have to be developed covering every aspect of the standards.

The full process of developing performance standards and sample assessment tasks will take approximately one and one-half years, assuming adequate resources and personnel. The resulting product — though ready for use — should still only be viewed as a beginning, to be improved upon over time.

Assessing the New Standards

• The standards should provide information on varying degrees of performance at grades 4, 8, and 12, each examination level.

• Assessment must be aligned with the new standards and sound instructional practices. For example, if we believe that we should be encouraging the development of extended mathematical reasoning and problem-solving, assessment must include complex tasks and ample time for thought. The importance of high quality assessments is further enhanced by the likelihood that high stakes incentives will be attached to performance on these measures.

- Assessment should focus on mathematical tasks for which students can train and do well, not "brain teasers" that require innate ability to perform successfully.

- We may wish to consider separable score results in a variety of mathematical "domains" to more fully capture the range of student math ability; this requires careful consideration to determine what new "domains" would be useful, if any.

- Assessment tasks should be written in a way that is understandable to a broad audience and past examinations should be made available for public review.

Raising Standards for American Education

Report of the Science Task Force

Background

The National Council on Education Standards and Testing was formed by the Congress and the President. The Council created five Task Forces in the core disciplines of English, mathematics, science, history, and geography plus three Task Forces to advise in the areas of standards, assessment, and implementation. The Science Task Force met at the Hotel Washington on October 15, 1991 from 10 a.m. to 5 p.m. The purpose of the Science Task Force is to advise the Council on the desirability and feasibility of national standards in science, and give the Council direction, if national standards are found to be desirable and feasible. To focus the task, copies of the following were provided to the Task Force: *Science Framework for California Public Schools* (California State Board of Education); *Science for All Americans,* (American Association for the Advancement of Science); *Earth Science, Content Guidelines, Grade K-12,* and *Earth Science Education for the 21st Century, a Planning Guide,* (American Geological Institute); and *1994 NAEP Science Consensus Assessment Framework Project,* (National Assessment Governing Board).

The views expressed in this appendix report reflect the work of this Task Force and are not necessarily those of the Council.

Status of Efforts to Develop National Standards in Science

The Science Task Force agrees that there is currently no set of content and performance standards that can be used as national standards. However, the National Academy of Sciences is spearheading a unified effort of numerous science organizations to develop national standards. In August, the National Academy submitted an unsolicited proposal to Secretary of Education Lamar Alexander and received initial funding to begin work on these standards. The National Academy has begun an analysis of current documents from the United States and other nations and is looking for common themes, content, and skills. By the end of 1991 the National Academy will have set up committees of science educators, teachers, administrators, state agencies, and the general public. Work on curriculum and learning outcomes will begin first. Development of teaching and instruction standards, (which includes discussion of instructional materials, opportunity to learn, and professional development) and assessment and performance standards will then occur simultaneously.

Are National Standards Desirable, Given the Wide Range of Student Performance?

Standards lend purpose to and reinforce the educational process. Standards can influence and improve science education and serve as the "glue" that holds together the education reform movement. Science teachers need to know what to teach. Nearly all elementary school teachers are responsible for science instruction, and they particularly need the framework that standards would give because they often have little or no background in science. National standards would improve instructional materials by the emphasis and direction they would give to publishers and instructional material designers.

Are Standards that Challenge All Children Without Penalizing Those of Lesser Opportunity Feasible?

The disparities in opportunity are in fact a most compelling argument for the importance of standards. Good standards used effectively can help reduce the disparities in opportunity. There must be good instructional models. Some districts need additional funding or a redistribution of funds so that every child can be challenged and helped to do her or his best and meet the standards. Issues such as lack of proficiency in English need to be addressed separately.

Who Should Develop the Standards and How Should They be Developed? What National, State, and Local Curriculum Materials Are the Best Available?

The Task Force believes that the major groups representing the science educational community are "getting together under the same tent" with the National Academy to develop standards. This process will also need to involve others, including school boards, school administrators, parent groups, state education and policy groups, state boards, lay persons, and business leaders. Science experts may take the lead to develop proposals that are presented to lay review groups. This dialogue should inform the public about the tough issues and, ultimately, about the decisions reached.

Looking at the best international, national, state, and local curriculum materials is an important part of the National Academy's work to develop standards. There is much available. The American Association for the Advancement of Science (AAAS) in *Science for All Americans* reports on literacy goals in science, mathematics, and technology. Several professional societies have completed projects that provide good source material, such as the American Chemical Society which has guidelines on chemistry for K-12, and the publication of the American Geological Institute titled *Earth Science, Content Guidelines, Grades K-12.*

How Long Will it Take to Develop the Materials? What Can Be Done to Expedite the Process?

By the fall of 1992, the National Academy of Sciences expects to have a draft of curriculum standards available for public scrutiny and debate. Consensus building will be the next step. Teachers must know and understand the process and recommendations. By 1994, the aim is to have content standards and soon thereafter assessment standards and a prototype of assessment tasks. The first assessments may be possible by 1995.

The National Assessment of Educational Progress (NAEP) will assess science in 1994 at grades 4, 8, and 12 using a new assessment now being developed. The National Assessment Governing Board (NAGB) already has adopted a content framework for the science assessment based on a national consensus process. The framework specifies the main topics to be tested, the relative weight for each, and the types of questions to be used. Later, after the assessment is constructed NAGB will set achievement levels for student performance. The NAEP science assessment will be completed largely in 1992 and early 1993 and will be available to the National Academy committees working on assessment standards.

The main way to expedite the standards development process is to expedite the funding. The initial funding for the development of science standards is available. Funding for the 1994 NAEP science assessment is appropriated, but funding for the National Academy standards development does not include assessment development. Efforts also need to be underway to develop teacher support, public support, and school board/district support.

The Task Force did not discuss the funding implications for implementing science standards across the nation. But a member noted that there are major costs involved in improving science education as this requires investment to develop "hands-on" materials, new forms of assessment, massive in-service teacher education, and new pre-service science curricula.

The "length of time to develop standards" does not address directly the issue of the time required to implement curriculum standards. There is debate over how soon new assessments of student performances can be used — that is how soon assessments can be used that are linked to new curriculum content standards that are being implemented. Several Task Force members suggested that assessments should follow the successful implementation of curriculum standards.

Other Issues

Clarification is needed in the area of Earth Sciences. This field is also in the geography curriculum in the United States and other countries. Possibly the geography community should be included as the science community discusses this area.

Technology is often linked with science, and there is continuing debate about the place of technology as a subject area in the science curriculum. Some contend that technology is a tool, albeit a powerful tool, for science, and others argue that the roles of science and technology are sometimes reversed. The Science Task Force certainly did not resolve this debate. In their brief discussion of technology, several Task Force members spoke of technology being built into the standards for teaching science rather than into the standards for science.

The primary purpose of assessment must be to improve learning. Imbedded assessment, where the teacher assesses during the learning phase, should be part of the process. Assessment must convey what the student can do and what the student has trouble doing.

Developing standards and assessments is a first step in determining what it takes to "get the standards to the student." We must give the teachers the support they need such as appropriate materials and staff development. School boards need to know what it takes to implement and meet standards.

Students need to learn both factual knowledge about the world around them and the reasoning and skills involved in "doing" science. This should not be viewed as an either/or question. As much as possible, students should gain the appropriate factual grounding in a manner that also teaches them to reason and investigate scientifically.

Report of the History Task Force

Background

The National Council on Education Standards and Testing was formed by Congress and the President. The Council created five Task Forces in the core disciplines of English, mathematics, science, history, and geography, plus three Task Forces to advise in the areas of standards, assessment, and implementation. The History Task Force met at the Hyatt Regency on October 23, 1991, from 10 a.m. to 5 p.m. The purpose of the History Task Force is to advise the Council in preparing its report. The Task Force was asked to respond to five specific questions relating to the desirability and feasibility of national standards in history, and to give the Council direction on the development of those standards, if national standards are found to be desirable and feasible.

Status of Efforts to Develop National Standards in History

The effort to develop national standards in history does not have to start from scratch but can build on previous work. There are a number of excellent documents already available: *History-Social Science Framework* (California State Board of Education); *Building a History Curriculum: Guidelines for Teaching History in the Schools* (Bradley Commission); *Charting a Course: Social Studies*

The views expressed in this appendix report reflect the work of this Task Force and are not necessarily those of the Council.

for the 21st Century (National Commission on Social Studies in the Schools); *Lessons from History: Essential Understandings and Historical Perspectives Students Should Acquire* (National Center for History in the Schools).

Also, the National Assessment of Educational Progress (NAEP) Consensus project in history will have content frameworks and test standards for testing on United States history in 1994 and world history in 1996.

Are National Standards Desirable, Given the Wide Range of Student Performance?

National standards would give guidance to teachers and to curriculum and textbook developers, and could help raise expectations in our schools if they are done the right way.

National standards should be voluntary. They should not be overly specific, but should present a core of agreement on what is essential. They should be flexible, leaving room for local history, divergent curriculum frameworks, a variety of textbooks, and various ways of teaching. National standards should have a global dimension and include world as well as United States history.

Are Standards that Challenge All Children Without Penalizing Those of Lesser Opportunity Feasible?

National standards can and must be fair, otherwise they will not survive the consensual development process nor be adopted by states and school districts. A test based on national standards will be fair because both educators and young people will know exactly what they need to learn to be successful on the test. Moreover, national standards will help the cause of equity by focusing attention on the need for equal resources to meet equal standards.

Studies show that children do not do well when their teachers have low expectations for them. All children have the right to aspire to the same set of goals, to be held to equally high expectations. National standards can thus be an instrument of equity by requiring all of us to do what it takes to educate all youngsters.

Who Should Develop the Standards and How Should They Be Developed?

National standards should be developed through a consensual process that allows various groups to be involved. The standard-setting process must be open and public. There must be several stages, so that the standards can be revised and refined in an iterative process. This process should involve teachers, professional organizations, groups with relevant expertise, and the public. There also needs to be some entity other than the federal government or any single professional association that brings all these groups together and coordinates the standard-setting process.

High quality national standards will result in assessments that include essays and open-ended questions, not just multiple-choice items.

National standards should allow students to demonstrate different levels of proficiency or achievement. The standards should also encourage interpretation and analysis as part of the study of history, not just the learning of basic facts.

History is an integrative field, since everything that has happened is part of history. National standards should be inclusive with regard to the content that can be taught in a historical framework, including civic education, economic history, art history, literature, geography, etc.

How Long Will it Take to Develop the Materials? What Can Be Done to Expedite the Process?

With appropriate resources, national standards could be developed within two years, perhaps sooner. It is vital to begin right away. Reading, writing, and mathematics assessment in NAEP are scheduled for 1993-94, and with geography and science moving forward as well, it is urgent to begin work immediately on history standards.

At some point there may need to be an entity, perhaps a quasi-governmental agency, to give standards efforts legitimacy and to provide an imprimatur for the standards developed by different disciplines. Schools and teachers need to know that there will be a long-term national commitment to the new standards.

Raising Standards for American Education

Report of the Geography Task Force

Background

The National Council on Education Standards and Testing was formed by the Congress and the President. The Council has created eight Task Forces to advise it on the best and most expeditious process to develop and implement standards in each subject area. Task Forces were created in the core areas of English, mathematics, science, history, and geography plus three others to advise in the areas of standards, assessment, and implementation. The Geography Task Force met on October 10, 1991, at the Hyatt Regency on Capitol Hill from 10 a.m. to 5 p.m. The purpose of the Geography Task Force is to advise the Council in preparing its report. The Task Force was asked to respond to five specific questions relating to the desirability and feasibility of national standards in geography and give the Council direction, if national standards are found to be desirable and feasible.

Status of Efforts to Develop National Standards in Geography

The Geography Task Force agreed that the work done by the National Council for Geographic Education (NCGE) and Association of American Geographers (AAG) called *Guidelines for Geographic Education*, which identified five fundamental themes in Geography and set up a sequence for geographic education, was an excellent

The views expressed in this appendix report reflect the work of this Task Force and are not necessarily those of the Council.

start toward the development of Content Standards in the field of Geography.

Outgrowths of *Guidelines for Geographic Education* are two documents published by the Geographic Education National Implementation Project (GENIP). These documents, *K-6 Geography* and *7-12 Geography* provide themes, key ideas and learning opportunities, which are grade level specific. There was consensus that this body of work is the best currently in the field in the development of performance standards. However, much more work needs to be done.

The Task Force agreed that the work being done by National Assessment of Educational Progress (NAEP) is the next major effort which will add to the development of content and performance standards in the field of Geography. NAEP will have initial work in Geography ready for publication in March or April of 1992. NAEP is using *Guidelines for Geographic Education* as one of its resources. NAEP and its governing board, NAGB, are working closely with the National Geographic Society as well as the major stake holders in the field of Geography.

The Task Force agreed that other important work is being or has been done by NAGB, the National Geographic Society, the Department of Labor's Secretary's Committee on Acquiring Necessary Skills (SCANS) Report, Careers in Geography, and the Geographic Alliance Network with AAG on their grant from the National Science Foundation. These efforts can be used in the development of geography standards.

The Task Force agreed that an important contribution is being made by Geographic Alliance Network, which was started by National Geographic Society and provides direct assistance for geographic education on a state-by-state basis. The Geographic Alliance was formed in response to a growing sense of alarm that our geographic illiteracy was hampering our competitiveness in international trade. The task of the Alliance is to revitalize geography with appropriate groups and re-establish its presence and importance in the curriculum. The infrastructure of the Geographic Alliance Network will be useful in disseminating information to members of the geographic community and to the public.

Are National Standards Desirable, Given the Wide Range of Student Performance?

The Task Force agreed that national standards are indeed desirable. The process of developing the National Standards will cause us as a Nation to identify what we believe to be important and permit the public and other stake holders to comment, scrutinize their efficacy, and help us as a Nation to identify and agree on national standards in geography.

Are Standards that Challenge All Children Without Penalizing Those of Lesser Opportunity Feasible?

The Task Force agreed that the standards must be set without regard to sociological or demographic factors. It is a grotesque disservice to the country and to the child to assume a child by virtue of his or her ethnic or socioeconomic background cannot achieve high standards. We assume every child can learn and accomplish high standards, with sufficient time to learn, tools, and resources. The standards themselves do not impose any penalties.

Who Should Be Involved in Developing Standards? Through What Process Should They Be Developed? What National, State, and Local Curriculum Materials Are the Best Available?

The Task Force agreed that the widest possible variety of stake holders should be involved in the process of developing standards including teachers, specialists, content area experts, pre-service teacher trainers, mass media, parents, business, legislators, textbook publishers, and possibly students. The question is the order in which they are to be involved. While there was some feeling that the "experts" (e.g. professionals in geography) should present the initial effort to be critiqued by the other groups, there was also sentiment that all stake holders should be involved in the up-front process from the beginning. Clearly, however, the professional development of teachers regarding the new standards and learning strategies to support those standards is a critical feature that must be included in the over all plan.

How Long Will it Take to Develop the Materials? What Can Be Done to Expedite the Process?

The amount of time necessary to develop standards is at least one year (December 31, 1992). This time line was given under the assumption that appropriate funding and personnel could be assigned to the task. We feel that this is a very optimistic time line.

Once the standards are released to the public and publishers, it probably takes 5 years to get a textbook series on the market. When the standards are in place there must be a concerted effort to get the information to the educational community and public. Appropriate learning strategies need to be identified and disseminated quickly.

The task force did not identify the "best" materials; instead, the task force acknowledged that the development of new materials which reflect the standards are another critical feature of the plan.

Standard-Setting Exercise

After an exercise in which the Task Force actually wrote some sample standards for the different grade levels, there was a general consensus that the use of the definitions of content, performance/ achievement standards was not completely clear. There needs to be more work and refinement on the definitions so that they are easily understandable. In fact, the use of "standards" following content, achievement, and performance (e.g. standards, standards, and standards) actually serve to confuse people who are reasonably expected to know something about their field. Many argued that the use of goals, objectives, and performance standards was clearer.

Further, it was difficult to set 8th grade standards, other than indicating that students should be expected to know more than they did in the 4th grade and less than the 12th grade.

Other Areas of Consensus

Debate occurred on whether geography was a separate or integrated discipline. There was consensus that the standards for the study of geography must be separated from the other disciplines. The result of imbedding it in other subjects is that only the understandings necessary for the other discipline are taught. It was believed that this has resulted in a lack of geographical understanding which has hampered the ability of our Nation to compete on the international market.

In some areas, the representative from the Business Round Table emphasized different points.

- The priority of business is not whether geography is taught as a separate entity, but that students understand practical concepts of geography that are useful knowledge to business.

- Business should be involved in the process of developing the curriculum from the beginning. Business prefers not to have a blueprint given to it to proofread after it has been developed. Business has been on the "steering committees" in the past; now it wants to be on the "working committees" with the content people and the teachers. Business wants the opportunity to react to (not set) standards at the time the standards are being considered.

- The business community realizes the problem of developing standards, but it would like to see the process time cut in the effort to get an initial product out quickly for public scrutiny.

The Task Force agreed that there is much that we can learn from the business community, and every effort must be made to incorporate them into the process.